TENNIS:
HOW TO PLAY, HOW TO WIN

Other books from Tennis magazine:

Tennis Strokes & Strategies
Instant Tennis Lessons

TENNIS:
HOW TO PLAY,
HOW TO WIN

By the **Editors** of Tennis magazine
and the **Instruction Advisory Board** consisting of
Tony Trabert, Roy Emerson, Vic Seixas,
Ron Holmberg, George Lott and Bill Price

A **tennis** magazine book

Published by Tennis Magazine
A New York Times Company
495 Westport Avenue
Norwalk, Connecticut 06856

Trade book distribution by
Simon and Schuster
A Division of Gulf & Western
    Corporation
New York, New York 10020

First Printing
ISBN: 0-914178-19-9
Library of Congress: 77-92906
Manufactured in the
    United States of America

ABOUT THIS BOOK

TENNIS magazine's Instruction Advisory Board (from left): Roy Emerson, Tony Trabert, Vic Seixas, Bill Price, George Lott and Ron Holmberg.

When you take a lesson from a tennis professional, does he sit you down and lecture you on the proper way to grip your racquet or where you should finish your follow-through? Of course not. He takes you out on the court and shows you.

That's what makes this tennis instruction book different and, we believe, more helpful than the others. Generally, they've tried to *tell* the reader how to play better tennis. Here, we *show* you—how to play and how to win. Much as a teaching pro would do, we demonstrate a complete stroke, isolate its vital components and then offer some key reminders at the end.

All of the material in this book originally appeared as monthly installments in TENNIS magazine's pioneering new Instruction Portfolio series. (The first series appeared in book form as *Tennis Strokes and Strategies*.) It took us fully three years to create and publish these Portfolios in the magazine. Now, they've been reviewed, reassembled and, in some cases, reworked to unite them in this new kind of instruction book.

Each chapter blends photographs, drawings and text to convey, simply and vividly, the mechanics of playing tennis successfully. All of the strokes—from the basic forehand drive to the sophisticated lob volley—are demonstrated in high-speed photo sequences that illustrate the full, correct motion for each of them. And key points are emphasized in large companion drawings. The strategy of the game is explained by the use of court diagrams that show players progressing through a number of typical points.

It's a uniquely graphic approach to instruction that

was developed by the editors of TENNIS magazine in collaboration with our distinguished Instruction Advisory Board. The board, established by founding editor Asher Birnbaum, participated actively in all the creative phases of the instruction that make up this book. Seldom, if ever, has so much collective expertise been brought to bear on the matter of how and where to hit a tennis ball. Between them, the six members of the board have won 59 major international singles and doubles titles and more Davis Cup matches than they can probably count. Just as important, moreover, they are all experienced and enthusiastic teachers of the game. The Instruction Advisory Board members are:

• Tony Trabert, who in 1955 won three of the major championships (the U.S., Wimbledon and French titles) and more recently has been U.S. Davis Cup captain, CBS television's tennis commentator and the overseer each summer of his own camp for juniors in Ojai, Calif.

• Roy Emerson, the ebullient Australian who has captured more major singles titles (12) than any man in history and served as coach of World Team Tennis' Boston Lobsters as well as Director of Tennis at The Registry Resort in Scottsdale, Ariz.

• Vic Seixas, the eternally youthful former U.S. and Wimbledon titlist who is still the No. 10-ranked senior player in the world and supervises the tennis program at the famed Greenbrier resort in White Sulphur Springs, W. Va.

• Ron Holmberg, a masterful touch player who was the No. 4-ranked American a few years ago, and who coached tennis at West Point and operates a summer camp for adults and juniors in Kent, Conn.

• George Lott, generally acknowledged to be the greatest doubles player the game has known (he won 11 U.S. and Wimbledon titles), who coaches at the club and college level in the Chicago area.

• Bill Price, a former table tennis champion who turned to tennis and developed such players as former Wimbledon champion Chuck McKinley.

These six fashioned the material in this book at annual winter meetings with the editors. (The editors, all of whom reside in the frigid reaches of Connecticut, saw to it that these meetings always took place at sunny, sybaritic tennis resorts in Florida or the Caribbean.) The daily sessions would begin each morning with spirited round-table discussions that were moderated by managing editor Jeff Bairstow and covered one or more instruction subjects. Art director Stan Braverman and sequence photographer Ed Vebell usually sat in, too. That way, they understood what would be needed when the board headed for the tennis courts after lunch to pose for the photography relating to the subjects that had been discussed. Afterward, the members of the board would play matches among themselves—and always attract a sizable group of spectators. After all, how often do you get a chance to watch four ex-Wimbledon champions in action on one court?

Later at the magazine's offices, Bairstow put together the Portfolios that comprise this book— working with transcripts of the roundtable discussions, the high-speed sequences and drawings provided by artist Red Wexler. Finally, before it could appear, each completed Portfolio was submitted to all the members of the board for their suggestions and comments. They had a few, you can be sure.

We think that their tennis knowledge and their involvement in this book come through, and that you'll find the pictorial format truly helpful. Because if you play tennis, or would like to, it's all here—from the rudiments of the game to the advanced refinements. It's our hope that this book will help you play better and win more often. But above all, we hope it will help you get all the fun out of tennis that there is for each of us.

—Shepherd Campbell
Editor, TENNIS magazine

CONTENTS

HOW TO HIT THE FOREHAND

The forehand is the most basic of all the shots in tennis—the workhorse stroke around which most average players build their games. It is generally the first stroke that novices learn and the one that many veterans depend on to see them through tough matches. The action of the forehand is a comfortable one for many players, partly because it so closely resembles another athletic motion that's familiar to them: swinging a baseball bat. But there are some distinctive and critical keys to hitting a forehand well. They are described and demonstrated in this chapter which is followed by a look at the other basic ground stroke, the the backhand.

1. Assume the ready position

When you're in the backcourt preparing for a
ground stroke—either forehand or backhand—
wait for the ball in a slight crouch similar to a
boxer's. Take a relaxed stance with your feet
spread at least shoulder-width apart, with your
knees bent and with a slightly forward lean of
your upper body. Get ready to spring into action
by bending enough to put your weight forward
on the balls of your feet, as Tony Trabert
demonstrates here.

Keep the racquet pointed straight ahead of
you, almost parallel to the ground, so that you'll
be ready to swing it the same distance for both
forehands and backhands. Cradle the throat of
your racquet with your other hand and you'll be
in a position to start your backswing.

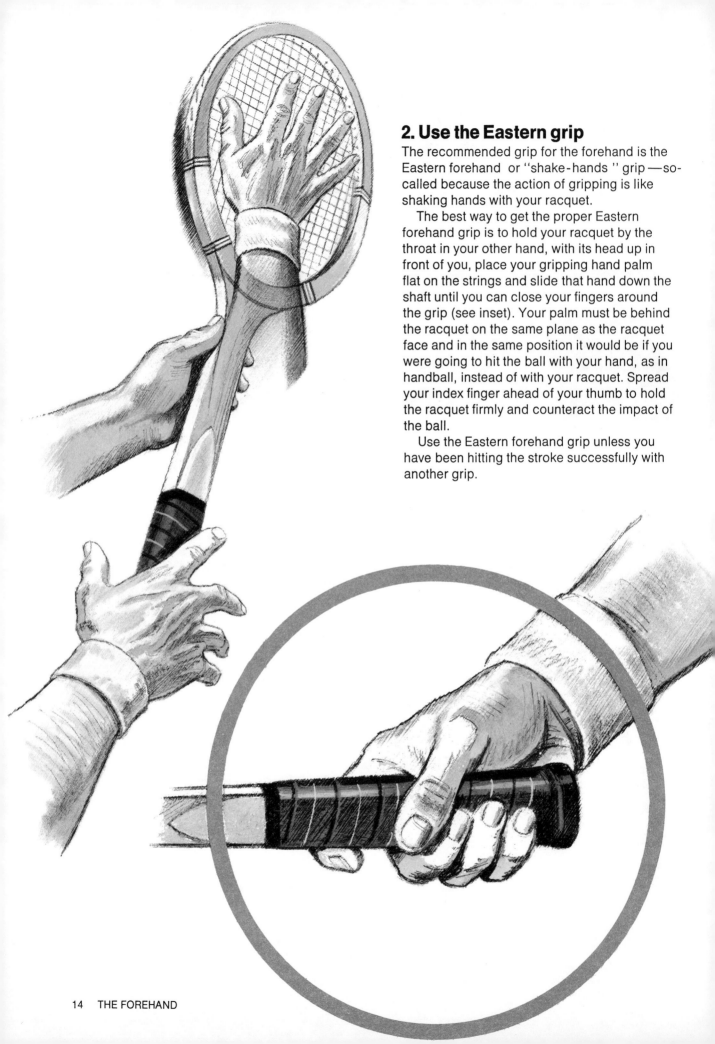

2. Use the Eastern grip

The recommended grip for the forehand is the Eastern forehand or "shake-hands" grip —so-called because the action of gripping is like shaking hands with your racquet.

The best way to get the proper Eastern forehand grip is to hold your racquet by the throat in your other hand, with its head up in front of you, place your gripping hand palm flat on the strings and slide that hand down the shaft until you can close your fingers around the grip (see inset). Your palm must be behind the racquet on the same plane as the racquet face and in the same position it would be if you were going to hit the ball with your hand, as in handball, instead of with your racquet. Spread your index finger ahead of your thumb to hold the racquet firmly and counteract the impact of the ball.

Use the Eastern forehand grip unless you have been hitting the stroke successfully with another grip.

3. Don't neglect the other hand

Use your other hand to cradle the throat of your racquet in the
ready position and, once you decide to take the ball on the
forehand side, to start pushing the racquet back as you begin
the backswing. Using your other hand at the beginning of the
backswing will force you to start the pivot of your upper body
and shoulders, which is one of the most critical parts of
forehand preparation (see the illustration on the next page).

Don't hold on too long, however. Simply release your other
hand when it feels natural.

Demonstrated by Tony Trabert.

4. Step toward the ball

As your body pivots and the racquet starts to swing back, head
toward the anticipated line of flight of the ball. First, swivel on
the balls of your feet and allow your weight to go into your back
foot so that you can push off hard. Then, move on your toes
with short, rapid steps.

Pause about a racquet's length from where you think the ball
will arrive and put your weight on the foot nearest the back
fence. You'll now be ready to push off for that final step into
the ball and put your weight into a powerful forehand.

5. Pivot your upper body first

The golden rule of stroke preparation is "get your racquet back early." As soon as you know that you're going to hit a forehand— even before you move your feet— turn your shoulders and hips to start your racquet hand going back. This upper-body pivot will put your arm and racquet in the right position for stroking almost immediately; that means if the ball comes upon you faster than you expect, you can still make a respectable shot.

As you pivot your upper body, your racquet will begin to go back and you can then continue the arm motion to complete the backswing. Of course, as you complete the pivot, you must start to push off from your back foot in order to get into position to hit the ball easily and comfortably. But remember: pivot first, step second.

6. Keep your racquet head up

Don't let the racquet dangle as you bring it back. Its head should be kept above the level of your wrist. If it droops below that point, you will be hitting under the ball with a weak and wristy shot.

Take your racquet back with the shaft either parallel to the ground or raised slightly, even more than Trabert's is here. And if you then swing forward the same way, you'll be more likely to hit a solid and deep forehand.

7. Swing the racquet straight back

The quickest way to get your racquet back is to use an almost level backswing so that the racquet ends up a little lower than the expected arrival point of the ball. That will enable you on the forward swing to come up into the ball and put a slight topspin on it.

If you use a large looping backswing, you'll bring the racquet up under the ball at a much steeper angle and are apt to hit a forehand that will look more like a lob. Also, the stroke will take more time.

So draw the racquet straight back as quickly and as smoothly as you can. Keep the racquet face vertical to the ground (not tilted forward in a closed position as Trabert has his racquet face here).

8. Get your weight back

When you move to the anticipated flight of the ball, pull up one step away from the hitting position and put as much weight as you can on your back foot. Then you'll be able to step and hit the ball, transferring all your weight forward as you make contact. Putting your weight into the shot will give your forehand power and depth. Get your weight back as soon as you pause for that final step to the ball.

9. Point your racquet at the fence

Finish your backswing with the racquet pointing toward the back fence. If you swing it back farther, you'll be bending your wrist and your stroke will be a wristy poke at the ball. Maintain a firm wrist because the forehand is basically an arm and a shoulder stroke with almost no wrist action.

If you have prepared early, you can keep your racquet pointing at the fence until the right moment comes to start the forward swing. If you aren't sure you are finishing your backswing correctly, have a friend check it for you and suggest adjustments until you stop at the proper point.

10. Step to the ball

As you prepare to hit the on-coming ball, step out with your front foot. That will begin the transfer of your weight forward so that as you meet the ball, you can get maximum power into the shot. Aim to place the forward foot out in front of you a bit so that you have a slightly open stance. That will mean you can rotate your body properly when you move the racquet around to meet the ball and, thus, put as much power as possible into the stroke. If you move the front foot directly forward, you'll have a closed stance which will cramp your swing.

11. Get your weight forward

As you begin the forward swing, have your weight on your front foot. The foot should be firmly planted, as Trabert's is here, with so little weight on your back foot that only the tip of the shoe is touching the court. Unless you are hitting a high forehand (see page 24), be sure to bend your knees so that you can get the racquet down to the ball without dropping the racquet head. And keep those knees bent through contact.

12. Grip the racquet firmly

To help you hit with control, tighten your wrist and grip as you swing toward the ball. Squeeze the racquet handle at this point and you'll feel your wrist tighten up automatically. Keep your grip tight through contact and into the follow-through. A firm grip will prevent the racquet from wobbling in your hand, which can only produce erratic shots. A firm wrist will help avoid the kind of flicking stroke that may be so weak the shot won't even clear the net.

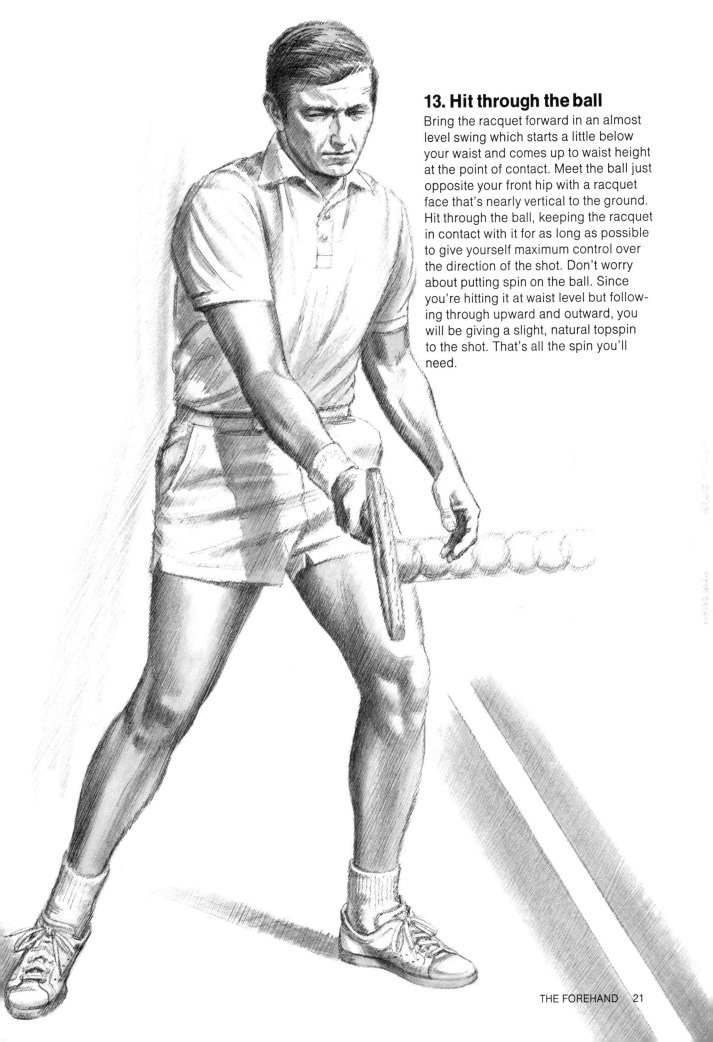

13. Hit through the ball

Bring the racquet forward in an almost level swing which starts a little below your waist and comes up to waist height at the point of contact. Meet the ball just opposite your front hip with a racquet face that's nearly vertical to the ground. Hit through the ball, keeping the racquet in contact with it for as long as possible to give yourself maximum control over the direction of the shot. Don't worry about putting spin on the ball. Since you're hitting it at waist level but following through upward and outward, you will be giving a slight, natural topspin to the shot. That's all the spin you'll need.

14. Control the direction

The placement of the shot will depend on the timing of your stroke in relation to your body. If you meet the ball squarely opposite your front hip, as Trabert does in this sequence, the ball will go straight ahead in a down-the-line direction. But you can send it crosscourt by taking it a little earlier out ahead of your front hip and then follow through.

15. Keep your eyes on the ball

Ideally, you should keep your eyes on the ball right up to the point where it hits the strings. Few players have the optical reactions to do that. But you should try and, at the very least, watch the ball down to the last couple of feet before impact. Concentrate so hard that you retain a mental image of the ball traveling those last few feet. If you're having trouble watching the ball, keep your head still like a golfer until after you've hit the ball. The better you follow the ball, the better your chances will be of hitting it in the sweet spot of your racquet.

16. Swing forward into your follow-through

As the ball leaves the strings of the racquet, follow through in the direction that you intend the ball to go. Swing out and forward as far as you can and the momentum of the motion will carry your racquet across your body so that it ends up pointing skyward on the other side. Since you'll be watching the ball as it flies over the net, you should be looking over your upper arm as you complete the follow-through. But don't stop to admire your shot. Resume the ready position and prepare for your next shot.

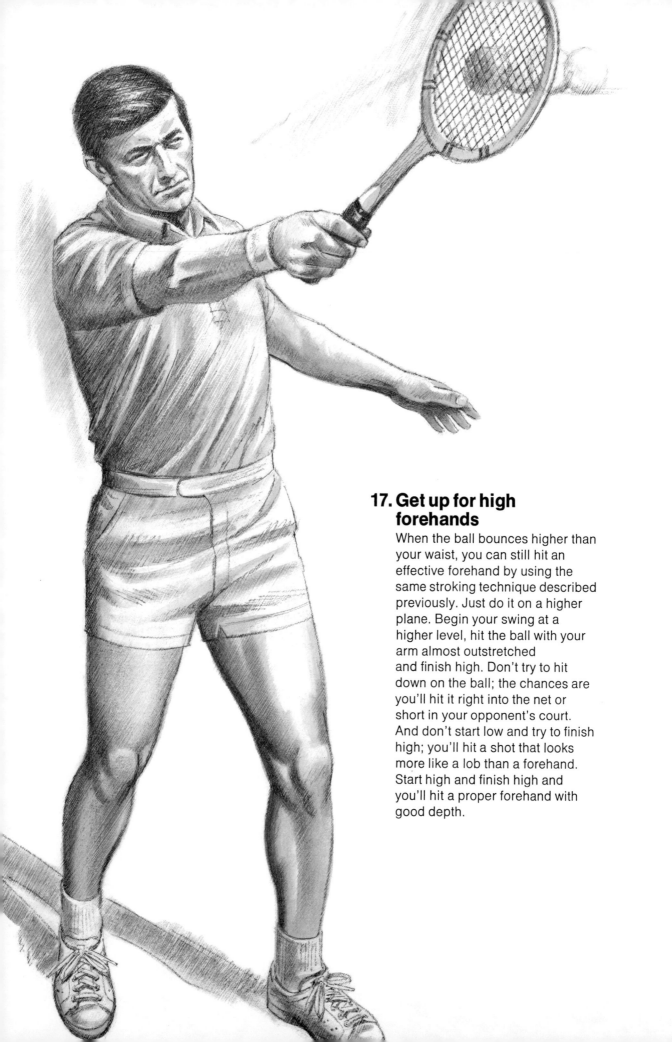

17. Get up for high forehands

When the ball bounces higher than your waist, you can still hit an effective forehand by using the same stroking technique described previously. Just do it on a higher plane. Begin your swing at a higher level, hit the ball with your arm almost outstretched and finish high. Don't try to hit down on the ball; the chances are you'll hit it right into the net or short in your opponent's court. And don't start low and try to finish high; you'll hit a shot that looks more like a lob than a forehand. Start high and finish high and you'll hit a proper forehand with good depth.

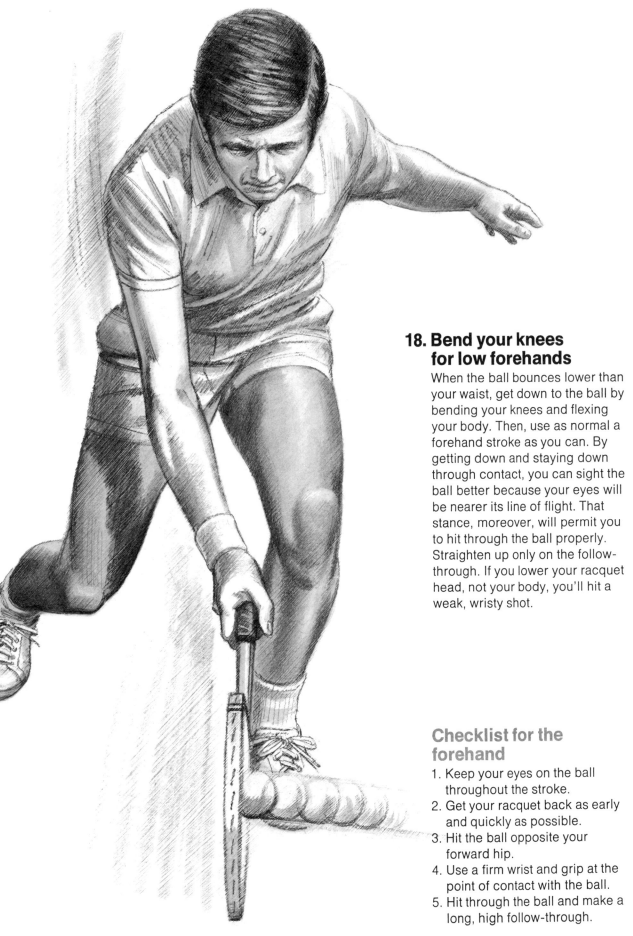

18. Bend your knees for low forehands

When the ball bounces lower than your waist, get down to the ball by bending your knees and flexing your body. Then, use as normal a forehand stroke as you can. By getting down and staying down through contact, you can sight the ball better because your eyes will be nearer its line of flight. That stance, moreover, will permit you to hit through the ball properly. Straighten up only on the follow-through. If you lower your racquet head, not your body, you'll hit a weak, wristy shot.

Checklist for the forehand

1. Keep your eyes on the ball throughout the stroke.
2. Get your racquet back as early and quickly as possible.
3. Hit the ball opposite your forward hip.
4. Use a firm wrist and grip at the point of contact with the ball.
5. Hit through the ball and make a long, high follow-through.

HOW TO HIT AN OVERSPIN BACKHAND

The backhand gives average players more trouble than probably any other stroke in the game. It's the novelty of the motion—hitting the ball on the other side of the body from the racquet arm—that accounts for much of the problem. If they are right-handed, players are conditioned to doing things on the right side of the body while the backhand, of course, is executed on the left side. But it's a problem that can be overcome, largely by proper preparation.

We recommend that players start with a natural overspin backhand—that is, one in which the player brings the racquet forward from a level below the ball's flight, swings through the ball on a slightly upward plane and finishes with a high follow-through. That gives the ball a forward rotation which helps send it deep and brings it down into the other court.

This chapter will also cover the underspin backhand and the two-handed backhand.

1. Make a decision

Both ground strokes—the backhand and the forehand—should begin from the same ready position. That's because you must be ready to prepare for a ball coming to either side. So the key is to make your decision to hit either a forehand or a backhand as soon as possible —preferably before the ball crosses the net. If your opponent hits a shot toward one of the corners, the decision is easy—you move toward that corner and take the ball on the closest side. But if the ball is coming more or less directly at you, then you should take the ball on your strongest side, whether forehand or backhand. Remember, though, to make your decision and your move as soon as possible.

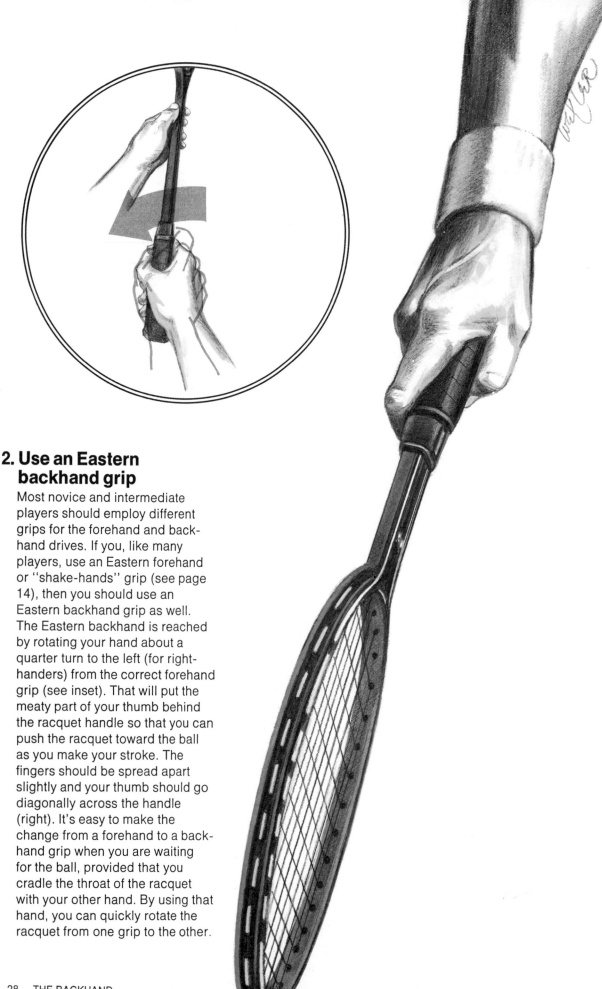

2. Use an Eastern backhand grip

Most novice and intermediate players should employ different grips for the forehand and backhand drives. If you, like many players, use an Eastern forehand or ''shake-hands'' grip (see page 14), then you should use an Eastern backhand grip as well. The Eastern backhand is reached by rotating your hand about a quarter turn to the left (for right-handers) from the correct forehand grip (see inset). That will put the meaty part of your thumb behind the racquet handle so that you can push the racquet toward the ball as you make your stroke. The fingers should be spread apart slightly and your thumb should go diagonally across the handle (right). It's easy to make the change from a forehand to a backhand grip when you are waiting for the ball, provided that you cradle the throat of the racquet with your other hand. By using that hand, you can quickly rotate the racquet from one grip to the other.

3. Get ready to move

In the ready position, take a relaxed stance with your
feet spread at least shoulder-width apart, your knees bent and
your upper body leaning slightly forward. Keep your weight on
the balls of your feet so that you will be ready to spring into
action as soon as your opponent returns the ball. Your racquet
should be pointed straight ahead, almost parallel to the ground,
and the throat should be cradled in your non-racquet hand.

4. Wait with the right grip

Many beginners wait on the baseline with a forehand grip
simply because their forehands are their stronger shots and
they hit most of their ground strokes as forehands. That means,
of course, that they usually have to switch grips to hit a
backhand. But as your game improves, or when you are facing
an opponent who is constantly attacking your backhand side,
you'll get a little extra edge by waiting with a backhand grip.
It's one less problem to think about as you take the racquet
back, and the time you gain will help you make a full backswing.

5. Rotate your shoulders

A cardinal rule for any ground stroke is to get the racquet back early. The sooner you do that, the more time you'll have to concentrate on meeting the ball and hitting it correctly. Get your racquet back fast by turning your shoulders as soon as you realize that you are going to take the ball on your backhand side. Rotate the upper half of your body so that it is sideways to the spot where you're trying to hit the ball. That will not only help you get your racquet back automatically but you'll also be better prepared to hit the ball if it comes up on you faster than you expect. Bring your front shoulder around so that it is almost pointing at the ball as it approaches. If you are a beginner, you should overemphasize the rotation to force yourself to turn quickly.

6. Use your other hand

Your other hand has two important roles to play in the backhand stroke. First, it helps you rotate the racquet so that you can get a proper grip. Second, your other hand helps you guide the racquet on the backswing. That means you'll be able to get your racquet back faster and will have better control of the racquet head. (In the sequence photos below, Trabert is keeping the racquet head slightly below his waist because he is anticipating a low bounce from the oncoming ball.) Keep your other hand on the racquet throat until you start the forward swing.

7. Take your weight back

As you prepare for a backhand, you should move with a few short, rapid steps to the ball, if necessary, so that you will be close enough to step toward it as you stroke. On your final step, you should lean into the ball so that you can put your weight behind the shot. That means that you must shift your weight back as you take your racquet back. When you complete your backswing, almost all your weight should be on your rear foot. Then you'll be able to step forward and your weight will go into the shot automatically.

8. Keep your elbow in

The racquet head should be brought back slightly below the level of the flight of the ball with the racquet handle almost parallel to the ground (see photo I). To do that, you must keep your elbow comfortably close to your body. If it protrudes out, your forearm will be pitched at an angle that will make it difficult on the forward swing to hit anything but a weak, flicking shot.

9. Face the ball

It's especially important to keep your eyes firmly fixed on the oncoming ball as you prepare for a backhand because the pronounced body rotation forces you to move your head, too. As your shoulders turn, keep your head facing forward so that you don't lose sight of the ball at any point. By watching the ball, you'll be better able to anticipate its flight and bounce and, thus, be in exactly the right position to make an effective shot. Good preparation means that your eyes must be ready, too.

10. Swing smoothly

Take your racquet back in one smooth swing. How you bring the racquet back is not as important as getting it back to give you room for a long, forward swing. Many players take their racquet arm back on an almost level path. For beginners, this kind of level backswing poses the fewest problems; there's little danger of the racquet going back too high and it's easy to keep the handle almost parallel with the ground. Some players, though, favor a slightly elliptical backswing in which the racquet head dips down and up. That's fine if the racquet head doesn't finish the backswing pointing up in the air. Whichever method you prefer, don't merely rotate your shoulders and then take the racquet the rest of the way back with a second action. Start the racquet back as you begin your shoulder rotation and keep it moving all the way back in one smooth movement.

11. Step toward the ball

If you prepare for the backhand properly by rotating your upper body and taking your racquet back, you will automatically transfer your weight to your back foot. Then, as you begin your forward swing, you should step toward the oncoming ball (see photo J below). That will do two important things to produce a solid shot: it will start you moving forward so you can put your body weight into the stroke; and it will help you get comfortably balanced.

J   K   L

12. Flex your body

As you start your forward swing, keep your knees bent and your upper body flexed. To hit a backhand with a little natural overspin, your racquet head must follow a slightly upward path to meet the ball. However, the racquet head must never be allowed to droop much below waist level. That means your body must be flexed so you can bend down, if necessary, to keep the racquet head just below the anticipated contact point. Flexing your body, moreover, will make it easier for you to move your body smoothly toward the ball.

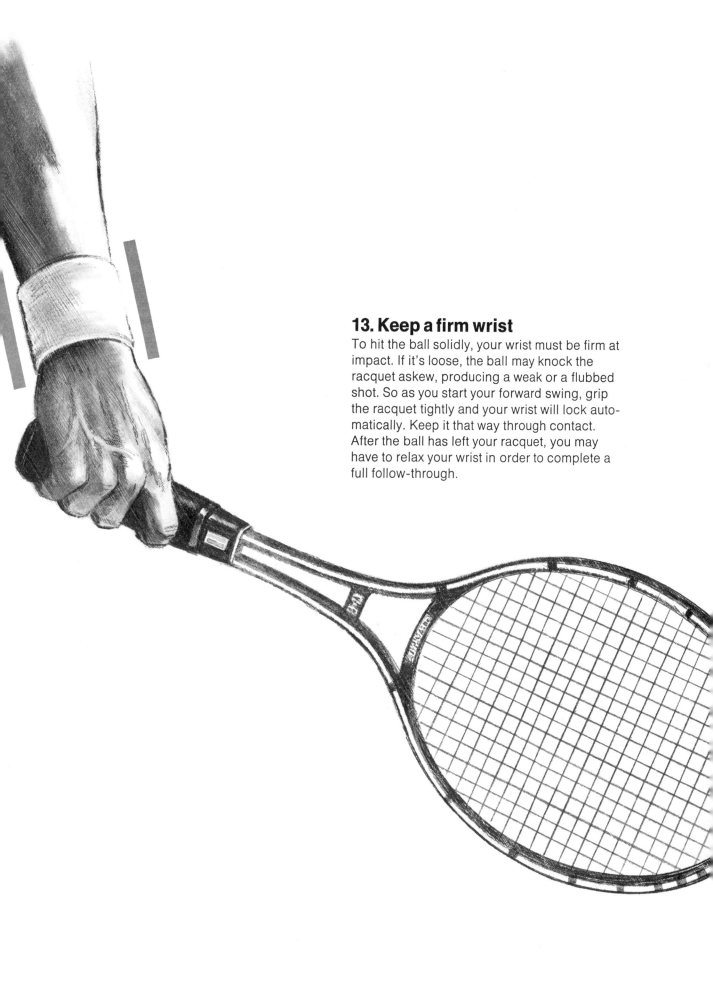

13. Keep a firm wrist

To hit the ball solidly, your wrist must be firm at impact. If it's loose, the ball may knock the racquet askew, producing a weak or a flubbed shot. So as you start your forward swing, grip the racquet tightly and your wrist will lock automatically. Keep it that way through contact. After the ball has left your racquet, you may have to relax your wrist in order to complete a full follow-through.

14. Bring your racquet up

The natural overspin backhand gets its spin from a slightly upward movement of the racquet through the hit. Before impact, your racquet head should be slightly lower than the ball's flight (see photo M below). As you move toward the ball, allow the racquet head to come up naturally so that you hit the ball in the center of the strings. Don't try to use your wrist to brush the racquet strings up and over the ball in an effort to impart extra topspin. That will only give you a shot with less power—unless you have an unusually strong wrist. Just swing up to the ball and let your racquet do its work naturally.

15. Watch the ball

Keep your eyes firmly fixed on the ball from the moment it leaves your opponent's racquet. Try to follow the ball right up to impact with your racquet. Unless you have remarkably good eyesight, it's unlikely you'll actually see the ball hit the strings. But you should be looking at the head of your racquet as you make contact out in front of your body. It doesn't matter if you momentarily lose sight of the ball immediately after impact. You'll have plenty of time to pick it up again as you go into the follow-through.

16. Hit through the shot

Meet the ball out in front of your forward foot. Your racquet should be moving on a slightly upward plane and the racquet face should be tilted back just a bit. Hit the ball solidly with a firm wrist and forearm. Don't pop the ball off the strings. Hit through it; in other words, keep the ball on your racquet strings for as long as possible. You should get the feeling of carrying the ball in the direction that you want it to go.

17. Uncoil like a spring

As you hit the ball, your front shoulder should whip around smoothly like a spring uncoiling. This uncoiling action will create racquet-head speed and, as a result, put power into the stroke. Think of the motion in terms of the way a baseball hitter brings both his shoulders and the bat around together to get maximum leverage in his swing. Then, come around and continue into your follow-through.

18. Finish your follow-through

Don't stop your racquet once the ball leaves your racquet. A racehorse doesn't pull up abruptly at the finish line; he goes all out to that point and then gradually decelerates. Similarly on your forward swing, move the racquet fast until you've hit the ball and allow the racquet to continue on out in front of you in the direction that you wish the ball to go. Let it slow down naturally as your body rotates and you follow through high and to the side. You'll now be facing the net, in position to watch the ball and prepare for your next shot. (See next page.)

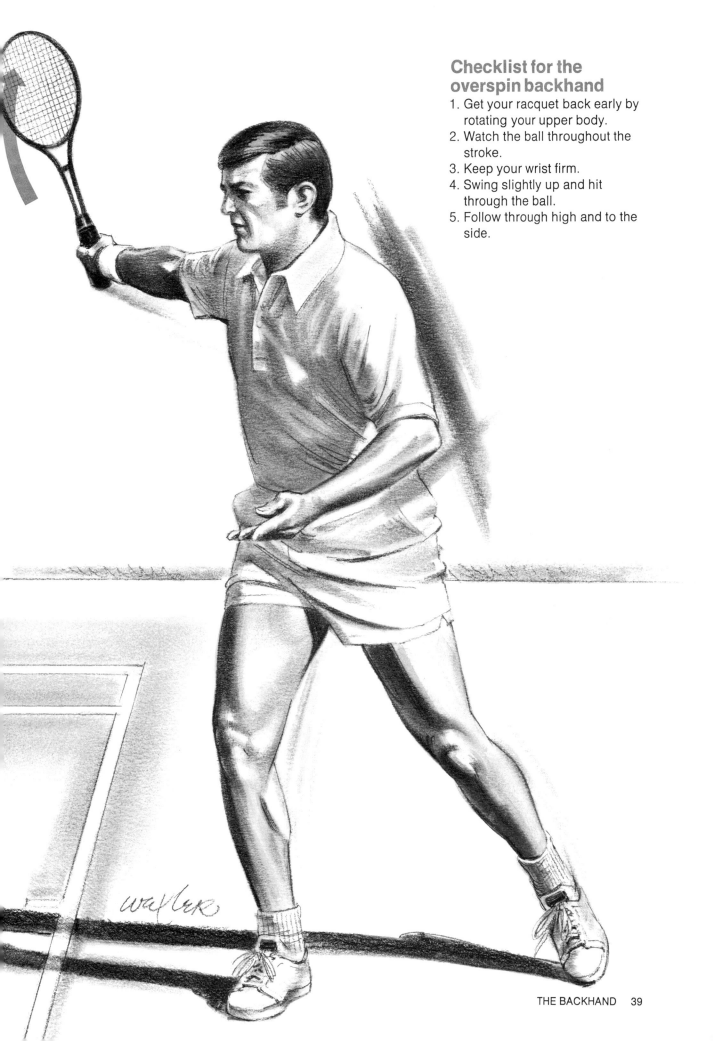

Checklist for the overspin backhand

1. Get your racquet back early by rotating your upper body.
2. Watch the ball throughout the stroke.
3. Keep your wrist firm.
4. Swing slightly up and hit through the ball.
5. Follow through high and to the side.

HOW TO HIT AN UNDERSPIN BACKHAND

Once you have developed a natural overspin backhand, you can extend your backhand skills with the underspin, or slice, stroke. Don't attempt to learn the slice shot first. Your backhand strength should lie in your conventional overspin stroke because that's a stronger shot. The underspin should be a refinement you call upon for variety.

Too many weekend players slice most of their backhands. The reason: they're late in preparing for the ball and have no choice except to swipe down on it. As a result, they have poor slices and nonexistent overspin backhands.

The underspin backhand generally travels low over the net and does not have the depth of an overspin shot because the underspin slows the ball down and produces little forward bounce (see illustration below).

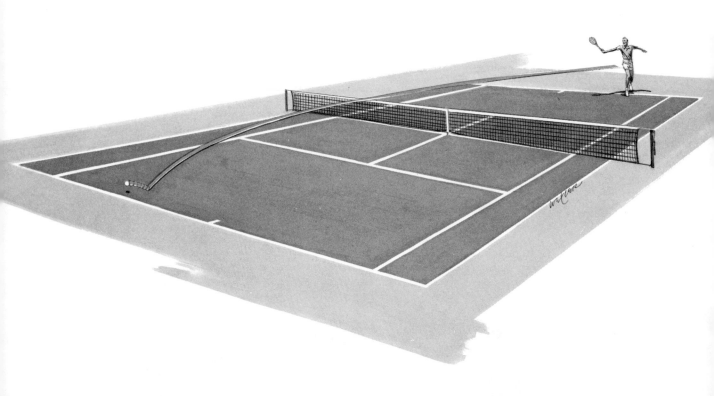

1. Modify your grip

To put underspin on the ball, you must take your racquet back relatively high on the backswing and then bring it forward and down to the level of the ball's flight. You brush your racquet strings slightly under the ball to produce the spin. All that is hard to do if you use the same full Eastern backhand grip that's recommended for the overspin backhand. Instead, you should adopt a Continental type grip which is about midway between the Eastern forehand and backhand grips. You can get a Continental grip by rotating your hand about one-eighth of a turn over the top of the racquet from the Eastern backhand grip. Or you can approximate the Continental by standing your racquet on edge and then grasping the handle from above.

Demonstrated by Vic Seixas

2. Lift your racquet

Your racquet must be brought down from above to meet the ball in order to put slice on it. So you should take your racquet back higher than you would for an overspin backhand. It's not important whether you use a looping backswing, as Vic Seixas is doing here, or a straight backswing. What is important is to take the racquet as far back as you can with comfort (photo C) and to keep the racquet head up. Your wrist should be held straight, although if you normally cock your wrist slightly on a backhand you can also do that on this shot.

3. Swing forward and down

Just as you do on a conventional backhand, you must swing forward with your weight behind the racquet to put pace on the ball. Don't simply make a chopping motion, bringing the racquet sharply down on the ball. If you do that, you'll put lots of spin on the ball; but it will have so little forward motion that, chances are, it won't get across the net. So you must swing your racquet forward as you swing down and you should step toward the ball to put your weight into the shot (photo E).

4. Watch the ball

The underspin backhand can be hit a little later than a normal backhand because of the angle at which the ball is struck. That means you must make an extra effort to watch the ball as closely as you can right up to the contact point (photo F). Be sure to hit the shot solidly in the middle of your racquet. If you tilt the racquet back too much or if you meet the ball off center, you're likely to hit a weak shot which may not clear the net or may present your opponent with an easy setup. So concentrate on the oncoming ball. It may help if you keep your eyes fixed on the contact point during and just after the hit; that will prevent you from pulling your eyes away before impact.

5. Drive through ball

As you meet the ball—that should be just in front of your forward foot—the downward motion of the racquet will provide the underspin. Your racquet face should be tilted back slightly, as Seixas demonstrates here, your body should be moving forward, your wrist should be locked, and your forearm and shoulder should be firm so that you can hit through the ball. Don't allow your wrist to droop; if the ball is low, bend your knees so that you are still hitting it with your racquet close to the level of your waist. The motion of your racquet should be from high to low. But don't let the ball pop off your racquet. Drive through the ball so that you have racquet contact for as long as possible.

6. Continue forward

To help you keep the ball on the racquet for as long as possible and to produce spin, you should keep the racquet going forward and down a little immediately after the hit (photo G). Let the racquet continue on its downward and forward push in the direction that you wish the ball to go until the natural motion of your arm causes you to bring the racquet up into the follow-through (photo H). By doing that, you avoid the temptation of bringing the racquet up too soon which would prevent you from putting the proper amount of spin on the ball.

7. Finish high

The natural momentum of your racquet arm in front of your body will carry your racquet from the low point after contact into a high follow-through. If you stop the racquet when it's down low in front, you'll have an abbreviated stroke. The racquet will probably be decelerating as you meet the ball, which means you'll hit a weak shot. By finishing high with a full follow-through, you'll be sure that you've driven through the ball. You'll then wind up facing the net, watching the flight of the ball, and be in good position to move for your next shot. (See illustration next page.)

Checklist for the underspin backhand

1. Use the Continental grip.
2. Lift the racquet on the backward swing.
3. Swing down and forward.
4. Watch the ball.
5. Hit through the ball.
6. Finish high.

HOW TO HIT THE TWO-HANDED BACKHAND

Never before has an unorthodox tennis shot gained such sudden popularity as the two-handed backhand has in recent years. It owes part of its new vogue, of course, to such stars as Jimmy Connors, Chris Evert and Bjorn Borg, who have stroked their way to the top of the game with it. But it has other attractions, too. The second hand on the racquet gives inexperienced or weaker players added support and power. And the second hand permits better players to change the direction of a shot later in the swing, which means they can disguise the stroke better.

There are, though, some real disadvantages to the two-handed backhand. The reach is more limited—and to compensate for that, faster footwork is required than on the one-handed shot. It also seems to encourage many beginners to slap at the ball rather than swing through it to get the control they should have. Thus, we suggest that you use a conventional backhand if you can and concentrate on improving that shot.

But if you prefer to use two hands, or if your backhand is truly weak, then this chapter will show you how to hit the two-handed shot effectively.

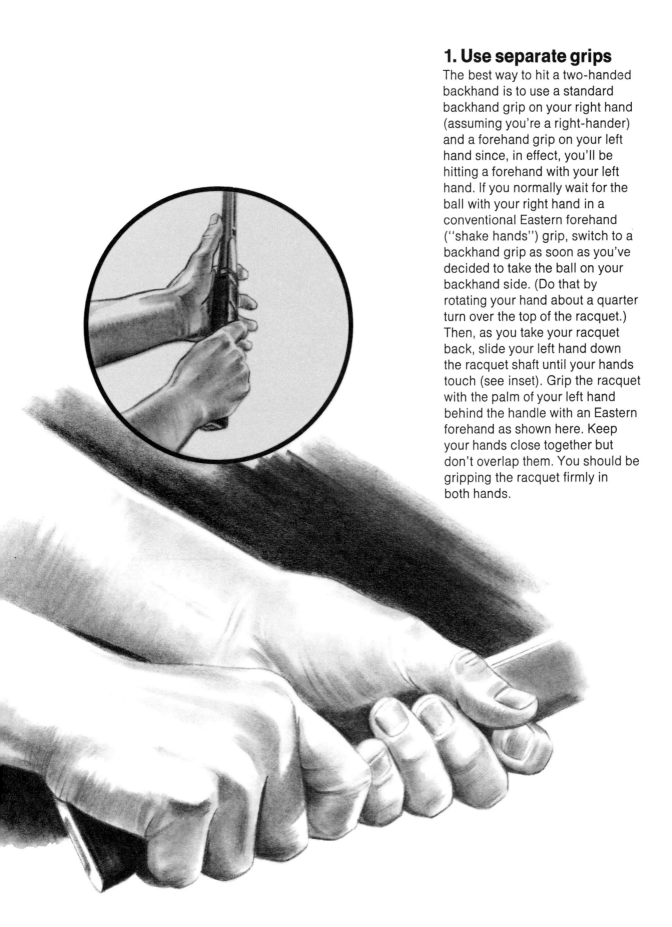

1. Use separate grips

The best way to hit a two-handed backhand is to use a standard backhand grip on your right hand (assuming you're a right-hander) and a forehand grip on your left hand since, in effect, you'll be hitting a forehand with your left hand. If you normally wait for the ball with your right hand in a conventional Eastern forehand ("shake hands") grip, switch to a backhand grip as soon as you've decided to take the ball on your backhand side. (Do that by rotating your hand about a quarter turn over the top of the racquet.) Then, as you take your racquet back, slide your left hand down the racquet shaft until your hands touch (see inset). Grip the racquet with the palm of your left hand behind the handle with an Eastern forehand as shown here. Keep your hands close together but don't overlap them. You should be gripping the racquet firmly in both hands.

2. Take a long backswing

As you take your racquet back (frame B above), you'll find that there's a tendency to use a short backswing because of the cramped position of the left arm. But a shorter backswing usually results in a less powerful shot. So you should try to take the racquet as far back as possible (D). Rotate your upper body so that your front shoulder comes around and your rear shoulder moves out of the way to let your left arm and the racquet go all the way back, as Trabert demonstrates.

Some top players take the racquet back with a looping motion. But, as with a conventional backhand, it's best to use a straight backswing since that's a simpler action—unless you already have a natural looping motion.

Take the racquet back until it is just a little lower than the anticipated flight of the ball. That way, the racquet will be rising as you hit the ball, which will provide a little natural topspin.

3. Hit firmly through the ball

You should make contact with the ball on a two-handed back-hand like a left-handed baseball player swinging at the plate; hit firmly through the ball so that you drive it deep into your opponent's court. Your arms should be straight and your wrists firm as you hit the ball.

Make contact about waist high—close to or a little in front of your front knee—and force the head of the racquet to follow the path of the departing ball. That will help you keep the ball on the racquet for as long as possible. Resist the temptation to overuse your left hand so that you slap at the ball. A slap shot may get you out of trouble occasionally, but you'll find the stroke will be erratic.

Your weight should be moving forward as you hit the ball so you can put maximum power into the shot. As the ball leaves your racquet, all your weight should be on your front foot; but you shouldn't be leaning so far forward, of course, that you lose your balance.

4. Watch the ball

Like a good golfer, you should keep your head down after you hit a two-handed backhand (frames G and H). Force yourself to look at the point where the racquet has just made contact with the ball. If you get in the habit of doing that, you'll remember to watch the ball all the way to the racquet.

Many players take their eyes off the ball just before contact because they are anxious to see what their opponents are doing. Don't watch your opponent! Make your decision about where to hit the ball before it arrives so that you can watch it continuously until after it leaves your racquet. Keeping your head down after contact will remind you to watch the ball—not your opponent.

5. Follow through completely

Many two-handed players are inclined to be lazy on the follow-through. That's a mistake that soon develops into a bad habit and results in weak and shorter shots. Finish your follow-through by rotating your upper body so that your rear shoulder comes around and points toward the departing ball. That will sustain the rising circular motion of the racquet that carries it to a finishing point high in the air on the opposite side of your body. A full follow-through will also help you to keep the racquet moving upward slightly as you hit the ball, an action that will add some natural topspin to your shot.

Checklist for the two-handed backhand

1. Watch the ball, not your opponent.
2. Get into position quickly and take your racquet well back.
3. Keep your forward arm straight and your wrists firm as you make contact.
4. Swing on a slightly upward plane and hit through the ball.
5. Finish your follow-through high and on the opposite side of your body.

THE SERVE

HOW TO SERVE EFFECTIVELY

When you're serving, it's the only time that you are in complete command, the sole master of your fate on the court. You're not responding to a shot hit by your opponent; you're initiating the action. And the outcome of the point that follows will depend, to a great extent, on how well you execute that serve.

There are three important types of serves—the slice (page 60), and the flat and twist serves (page 70). Each has its special uses. But to be effective, each depends on one critical thing: an accurate ball release. So in this chapter, we'll first show you how to place the ball in the air properly before moving on to the three different types of serves.

Release the ball

The key to a good serve is the ball release—the placement of the ball in the air consistently at the point where you can hit it most effectively. Very little arm speed is needed to place a two-ounce ball a few feet up in the air. So don't think of the action as a ball toss but, instead, as a ball release. If you toss the ball, it will be difficult to place it in the right spot each time. Aim to develop just enough arm momentum so that the ball leaves your fingers smoothly and gently with no arm, wrist or finger snap which can produce an erratic motion.

1. Take the proper stance

When serving, first assume a comfortable, relaxed stance just behind the baseline. Stand with your feet about shoulder-width apart, your front foot placed at about 45 degrees to the baseline and your weight on your back foot. You should be sideways to the net so that a line drawn from toe to toe would point directly to the court where you're about to serve. Position your feet this way whether you are serving close to the center mark, as in singles, or between the center mark and the singles side-line, as in doubles. Remember, too, to keep your front foot about three or four inches behind the baseline so you don't foot fault.

2. Start with two

Since you get two serves on each point (or more if a let ball lands fair), it's best to begin by holding two balls. That way, if your first delivery is a fault, you can serve again without fumbling around for a second ball and, perhaps, spoiling the rhythm of your motion. If your first serve is successful, you can either hang onto that second ball or throw it behind you if you need both hands to hit a two-handed shot. Of course, if your opponent is distracted by the action of casting that second ball aside, you may have to serve with only one ball.

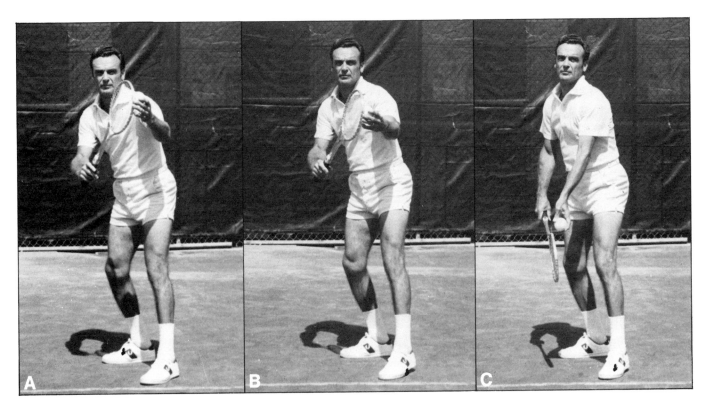

3. Hold the ball lightly

By taking two balls in your hand, you will be forced to hold the ball you are about to serve on the tips of your fingers and thumb the way you should. Cradle the ball so lightly that another player could pluck it out of your hand with no resistance. Place it atop your thumb and first two or three fingers. If you have to use a second ball, push it up into the same position on your fingertips where you had the first ball. With the ball held properly, place the racquet and ball out in front of you about chest high. Then, drop both arms together toward your front knee, as Seixas demonstrates here.

4. Place it out in front

For consistency, move your ball arm up in a straight path each time. It should come up out in front of you and to the right (for right-handers). Lift the ball in as straight a vertical line as possible. Your objective is to position the ball so that if you were to let it drop without striking it, it would fall out in front of you and to the right of your forward foot. Don't release the ball directly overhead; remember, you want to hit it out in front, so place it out in front.

5. Move both arms together

As you bring your ball arm up for the release, you should also be moving your racquet arm back and up in preparation for the racquet's rendezvous with the ball. If you have trouble coordinating the release with the hit, try this counting system. Start with the racquet and ball at chest level. On the count of "one," both hands go down. On the count of "two," both hands go up—the ball hand in front and to your right and the racquet hand behind you. On the count of "three," hit the ball.

6. Open your fingers

Release the ball at the point where your arm is no longer able to continue up in a straight vertical line. For most players, that happens when the arm reaches a point between the level of the shoulder and the top of the head. Release the ball with an almost imperceptible opening of your fingers as though you are pushing the ball into the air. Your ball arm should continue on up slightly after the release and then fall to your side.

7. Place the ball at the tip of your racquet

Lift the ball in the air so that, at its apex, it's about as high as the tip of your racquet when your arm and body are fully extended. You want to contact the ball just as it descends from the top of its rise where it will be barely moving and, thus, be easier to hit. If you place the ball too low, your arm action will be cramped and you'll hit a weak serve that will, most likely, be a fault. If you place the ball too high, you'll have to wait for it to come down before you can make contact. That will do more than disturb the rhythm of your serve. You'll also have to hit the ball as it falls, which is harder than hitting a barely moving ball.

8. Practice your release

The ball release is one tennis motion that you can practice at home by yourself. You can even practice indoors—in your garage, basement or anyplace with a ceiling higher than the maximum height of your release. Hang a small object—another tennis ball will do nicely—from the ceiling so that it is just above the point you can reach with your body, arm and racquet fully extended. Then, practice releasing the ball so that it barely touches the suspended object. Keep trying until you can hit the same point at least nine times out of 10.

Checklist for the ball release

1. Hold the ball lightly in your fingertips.
2. Release the ball so it rises in front of your forward foot and to the right.
3. Let go of the ball by opening your fingers gently.
4. Place the ball in the air only as high as the point you can reach with the tip of the racquet when your arm and racquet are fully extended.

HOW TO HIT A SLICE SERVE

Of the three major types of serves—the slice, the flat and the twist—the slice is the one that the average player must rely on much of the time. It can be used on the first and the second serves, in singles and doubles and it will almost always keep the receiver guessing. So it's a weapon every player should work on mastering.

TWIST

Slice for safety

A flat serve, which has almost no spin (center), takes a nearly straight path through the air and, on most surfaces, bounces relatively low. The chance of making an error with the flat serve is high since the ball must skim close to the top of the net in order to land inside the service box. A slice serve, which has sidespin (right), is inherently safer since it curves into the service box. It's slower than a flat serve but breaks away from a right-handed receiver (in the deuce court), making his return more difficult. A twist serve, which combines sidespin and topspin (left), passes high over the net, drops sharply into the service box, and on most surfaces kicks high into the air after the bounce. The twist serve is difficult to execute but, done correctly, is a safe serve which gives receivers some problems.

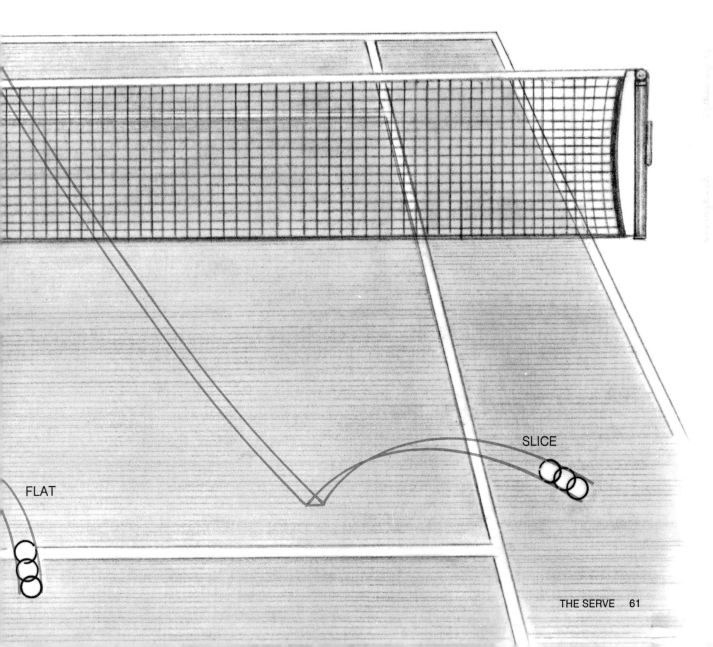

FLAT

SLICE

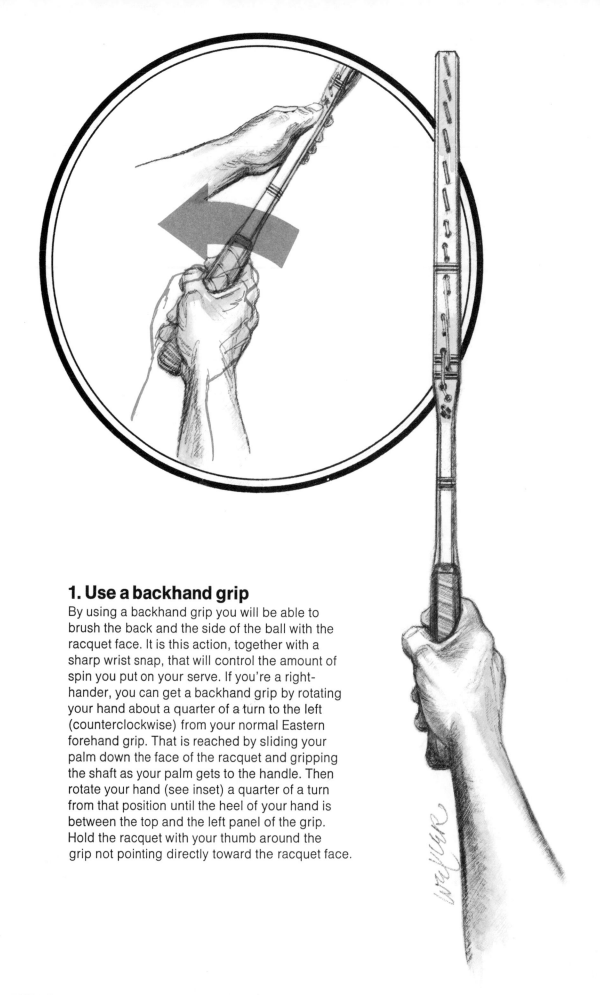

1. Use a backhand grip

By using a backhand grip you will be able to
brush the back and the side of the ball with the
racquet face. It is this action, together with a
sharp wrist snap, that will control the amount of
spin you put on your serve. If you're a right-
hander, you can get a backhand grip by rotating
your hand about a quarter of a turn to the left
(counterclockwise) from your normal Eastern
forehand grip. That is reached by sliding your
palm down the face of the racquet and gripping
the shaft as your palm gets to the handle. Then
rotate your hand (see inset) a quarter of a turn
from that position until the heel of your hand is
between the top and the left panel of the grip.
Hold the racquet with your thumb around the
grip not pointing directly toward the racquet face.

2. Hold your racquet up

The proper starting position for the serve is a few inches behind the baseline—to avoid foot faulting—with your front foot placed at 45 degrees to the baseline and your feet spread comfortably about shoulder-width apart. Start by bringing the racquet and ball up and out in front of you to about chest level. Most players touch the racquet and ball together to help start the rhythm of the service motion. As you bring the racquet up in front of you, check the service box that you are about to aim for and make sure that your opponent is ready to receive serve. Some players bounce the ball before serving. There's nothing wrong with that but it's not necessary and it can be a distracting or delaying tactic. All you need to do is get set and serve.

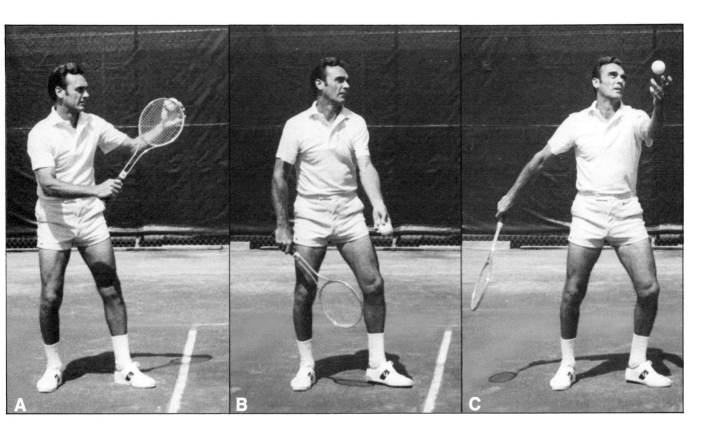

3. Try the countdown system

Many players have trouble coordinating the ball release and the hit. If you are having that problem, this countdown system may help. On the count of "one," both your arms should go down. On the count of "two," your ball arm should come up in front of you and your racquet arm behind you like a bird spreading its wings. On the count of "three," your racquet should come up and forward to hit the serve. Count "one, two, three" for the drop, the lift and the hit. You'll find that the count will help you develop a smoother and more coordinated serve.

4. Get your elbow high

To put some power into a slice serve, you must take the racquet back as far as possible. Not all players can get the racquet into a backscratching position and, indeed, that exaggerated motion is not absolutely necessary. You'll get the racquet back far enough— and your wrist properly cocked— if you lift your elbow up as you take the racquet back. When the racquet is back and your elbow is high, you'll be ready to bring the racquet forward with a throwing action that will put power into your serve. Get your elbow high and the racquet and wrist positions will take care of themselves.

5. Flex your body

You don't need a muscular build to hit a strong serve. You can use your body weight to help put power in the shot. Think of your body as a coiled spring about to be unleashed when you hit the serve. That means you should bend your knees and flex your body as you prepare to hit the serve. Then, as your racquet begins to move forward, uncoil your body to get maximum power into the stroke. Stretch upward as your racquet moves upward and you'll feel the uncoiling action adding power to your serve. You'll also hit the ball higher in the air which will make for a better serve.

6. Move your weight forward

When your racquet's back in readiness for the hit, your weight should begin moving from your back foot onto your front foot. This weight transfer will enhance the uncoiling action of your body. The weight transfer should be continuous so that your weight will keep going forward as you move into the follow-through. If you do it correctly, you will be forced to take at least one step into the court either to maintain your balance or to start your run up to the net.

7. Throw your racquet

From the backscratching position, the racquet has to accelerate sharply on the forward swing. You can get this rapid acceleration by bringing the racquet forward as though you were trying to throw it over the net. In fact, some instructors teach beginners this action by having them actually toss an old racquet as far as possible. If you are used to throwing a baseball or football overhand, you'll easily develop the throwing action for the serve. If not, practice throwing a racquet a few times until you get the feel of the snapping motion that's involved.

8. Keep your head up

It's just as important to keep your eyes on the ball when you serve as it is when you hit any other stroke. Watch the ball as you lift it into the air and keep watching it intently as you hit it. If you lose sight of the ball before you make contact, that may be because you are dropping your head as you bring your body forward. If you force yourself to keep your head up and your eyes glued to the ball, you'll increase your chances of hitting the ball squarely in the center of your racquet. And, of course, you'll be better able to continue watching the flight of the ball as it goes into your opponent's court.

9. Snap your wrist

As you bring the racquet forward, your wrist should stay in the cocked position it assumed when it was behind your back until the racquet head is within a few feet of the ball. At the last moment, you should snap your wrist forward so that your forearm, wrist and racquet handle form an almost straight line on contact with the ball. The wrist snap imparts extra acceleration to the head of the racquet and, thus, helps you add power to the shot. The continuation of the wrist snap around the side of the ball will help put spin on the ball. So it's important that you snap your wrist as far forward as you can, continuing it into the follow-through.

10. Brush the ball for spin

To put spin on the ball, the racquet must make contact at the back of the ball and continue that contact around to the side as you complete the hit. If you use a backhand grip, your wrist snap will almost force you to brush the back and side of the ball as your wrist straightens out. If you fail to move the racquet head around the ball, you'll hit a flat serve with little or no spin. The more you brush the ball, the more spin you'll put on the ball. To get the racquet to move across the back and side of the ball, a right-hander serving into the deuce court should swing as though he's aiming at the right-hand net post. If he meets the ball correctly, that racquet motion will still cause the ball to go into the proper court.

11. Finish the follow-through

The serve does not end when you hit the ball. You should complete your delivery by bringing the racquet around to the opposite side of your body in a full follow-through and by taking at least one step into the court. If you don't have a complete follow-through, the chances are that you are slowing down your racquet as you make contact and, as a result, hitting relatively weak serves. Follow through so that your racquet comes to rest behind you pointing to the back fence.

Checklist for the slice serve

1. Make sure you're using a backhand grip.
2. Take your racquet well back and keep your elbow high.
3. Watch the ball by keeping your head up.
4. Snap your wrist as you hit the ball.
5. Complete your follow-through across your body.

TWIST   FLAT

HOW TO HIT THE FLAT AND TWIST SERVES

Once a player has mastered the basic serve—the slice—he can add dimension to his game by developing the other two types of serves—the flat and twist. The flat serve is a powerful shot hit with almost no spin. It takes an almost straight path through the air and, on most surfaces, bounces low. The flat serve is used mainly as a first serve when the server is trying to ace his opponent.

By contrast, the twist serve has both side-spin and topspin and curves into the service box, often kicking away from the receiver. The twist serve, thus, is a good second serve when hit correctly. However, the twist serve is relatively difficult and should not be attempted until you've learned the slice.

1. Where to place the ball

The ball release for the flat serve is almost the same as for the slice serve. Place the ball out in front of you and to your right (for right-handers). Lift the ball gently (right) so that if it were allowed to drop, it would land in front of you to the right of your forward foot.

For the twist serve, however, you should place the ball slightly to your left because you will have to snap the racquet up and over the ball to impart the proper spin. Lift the ball in the air (left) so that if it were allowed to drop, it would fall to the baseline. Don't place the ball quite so high in the air as you would for a slice or flat serve, though, because the contact point for the twist should be a bit lower.

2a. Starting the flat serve

A flat serve should be hit as hard as possible so you ace the shot or at least force a weak return. For that, you must have a smooth swing and put your body weight into the shot. Start with the racquet and ball held in front of you at about chest height (A). Use the downswing of both arms (B) to start a rhythmic action. You'll put your body weight into the shot if you lift the ball into the air well in front of your body (C) and stretch upward and outward to make contact. As you release the ball, your racquet should come up smoothly behind you.

2b. Starting the twist serve

The start of the twist serve should look as much like a slice or flat serve as possible so you don't telegraph your intention to your opponent (J). However, to impart the spin required for a twist serve, most players should lift the ball closer to the body (K, L) than for a flat or slice serve (see above). Place the ball above your left shoulder and only a couple of inches in front of your body. As the ball leaves your fingers, bend your knees and begin to coil your body to prepare to hit up and over the ball.

3a. Stretch your body for the flat serve

The motion of hitting a flat serve is almost like that of the slice except for the movement of the racquet immediately before and after impact. To slice a serve, the racquet must go around the ball to impart the spin. For a flat serve, the ball must be hit squarely from behind without any attempt to put spin on it. The key to the flat serve is power. To get that power, you should coil your body (D) as you take the racquet back so that you can uncoil like a spring as you stretch into the hit. Take the

3b. Bend your back for the twist serve

The twist serve is not an easy stroke. You must put topspin and sidespin on the ball so it will bounce high in the air and be difficult for the receiver to return. To get the required spin, the racquet must go up and over the ball at contact. That calls for a pronounced wrist snap and a hitting position different from the one used for the slice and flat serves. However, the early part of the racquet motion is identical to the other two serves. Take the racquet back smoothly as far as you can (M). Flex your

racquet as far back as possible (E) so that your forearm is
parallel to the ground. Bring the racquet up and forward with a
throwing action (F) directly behind the ball. Stretch up and
forward to hit the ball in front of you with your body and
racquet arm fully extended (G). Put your body weight into the
shot so that you are forced to take one or two steps into the
court (H) after the hit. Complete the stroke by following through
fully (I) without any interruption in your swing. After hitting a
flat serve, start your run up to the net.

body by bending backward like an archer's bow (N) and get
your weight well back. Then, bring the racquet up smoothly
and snap your wrist through the hit (O, P) so that the racquet
hits the ball with almost an upward blow. There should be
some forward motion, of course, but most of your effort
should go into snapping the racquet to put spin on the ball.
After contact, your racquet should continue out in front (Q) and
to your right (for a right-hander). Finally, follow through
completely and finish with your racquet on your left side (R).

4a. How to put power into a flat serve

The key to getting speed on a flat serve is to put all your body weight into the shot. By lifting the ball well in front of your body, you will force yourself to hit it out in front and, thus, bring your weight through as you hit (left). It is also important to lift the ball high enough in the air so that your body is fully extended with your arm straight at contact. A cramped action will not allow you to get your weight into the shot. Meet the ball directly from behind (see inset above), hitting out with an almost vertical racquet face. If you hit down, the ball will go into the net. Since you cannot hit a ball in a straight line and expect it to go into the service box, you'll have to rely on gravity to pull it down. However, if you hit the ball up, the serve will go long. That's why there is a fair amount of risk involved in the flat serve. You should use it only as a first serve and avoid it on critical points.

Checklist for the flat serve

1. Lift the ball out in front and to your right (for a right-hander).
2. Uncoil like a spring as you stretch up to hit the ball.
3. Hit the ball in front of your body and bring your weight through as you hit.
4. Finish your follow-through across your body.

4b. How to get spin on a twist serve

When you hit a twist serve the racquet head has two motions—upward and forward. The upward motion comes from the snap of your wrist just before contact; the snap continues through contact and finishes just after the ball leaves your racquet. The forward motion comes from the forward movement of your arm and body as you swing your body weight through the hit. If you were to imagine a clock face on the rear of the ball, the face of your racquet should contact the ball at about the seven o'clock position and then brush sharply up and over the ball to the one o'clock position. You can do that only if you contact the ball at a slightly lower height than with a flat or slice serve. Don't contact the ball at too low a point, however, or you'll cramp your motion so much that you'll fail to get any power into the shot. The twist requires considerable practice. But once mastered, it's a useful second serve and occasionally a good surprise weapon as a first serve.

Checklist for the twist serve

1. Lift the ball in the air close to your body so that you can put spin on the ball as you hit.
2. Get your weight well back and flex your body before the hit.
3. Use maximum wrist snap to bring the racquet head up and over the ball as you make contact.
4. Finish your follow-through across your body.

HOW TO RETURN SERVE

The return of serve cannot be classified as a single, specific tennis stroke. Sometimes it's hit as a forehand, sometimes as a backhand and occasionally as a lob. Returning with those strokes, moreover, is often much more difficult than hitting them during a rally. After all, the server is in complete control of the situation, while the receiver is in a defensive position and must make some quick decisions about the speed and spin of the serve once it's delivered. Not surprisingly, the receiver may be apprehensive as he awaits the ball.

So it pays a player to familiarize himself with the basics of returning serve successfully —both from the stroking and the tactical standpoints.

1. Be ready, relaxed and alert

Most players feel some tension when waiting for a serve and, to dispel that, top players often shake an arm or a leg or twirl the racquet. It's a good idea to try to relax before you step up to receive serve. Then carefully take up your ready position on or near the baseline. Keep your racquet head up, your body flexed, your knees bent and your weight on the balls of your feet, as Ron Holmberg demonstrates here. Remember that this is the one time in a point when you can really get ready. Don't be rushed by the server; he has to make sure that you are all set before he serves.

If you normally prefer to receive serve on your forehand, wait with an Eastern forehand ("shake-hands") grip. An experienced player, however, will often attack your backhand with his serve. In that case, you might wait with a backhand grip—a one-quarter turn of the hand over the top of the racquet (see inset). It's just one less thing to think about as the ball whizzes toward you.

After you take up your ready position, concentrate on the server and on the ball that he's about to release. Ignore the other players and don't allow yourself to be distracted by anything going on cff-court. Always stay alert.

2. Move when the ball moves

When you are in the ready position (frame A, below), your movement to the ball will be delayed by your brain's reaction time and by your body inertia—or the time it takes to get your body moving. You can shorten your reaction time by watching the ball intently as it leaves the server's hand. Does the racquet hit the ball flat or at an angle? If it's at an angle, then you know that the ball will be sliced and you can drift sideways. If you can't judge the angle, use your ears. A ball hit flat will have a sharper sound than one hit with spin.

You can reduce the effects of body inertia by bouncing on the balls of your feet (B) as the ball is released. That way, you will be up and moving, ready to start your upper body turn (C) the moment you determine the ball's direction.

Demonstrated by Ron Holmberg

3. Get your racquet back early

On first serves, in particular, a receiver has less time for his shot than he does when hitting a normal ground stroke. That means you should both prepare quickly and take a slightly shorter backswing. Watch the server hit the ball so you can determine the direction of the ball immediately after it has left the racquet. Then, start turning your upper body (C) so the racquet starts its backswing at the same time.

Get through this stage of the stroke as fast as you can so your forward swing can be as complete as a conventional ground stroke. Take the racquet back as quickly as you can. If you normally have a looped backswing on your ground strokes, keep that loop compact.

4. Use a shorter backswing

When you are up against a fast server, you simply won't have enough time to react, take your racquet well back and hit the ball. So you'll have to shorten your backswing and concentrate on hitting through the ball. The key is to adjust your backswing to the server. If the serve is a real bullet, you may only have enough time to block the ball back. There's a trade-off here, of course. You can use the pace on a fast serve to hit an effective return though you may be forced to use a short backswing.

Conversely, on a slower second serve, you'll have enough time to make a complete backswing and, indeed, you'll most likely need that backswing so you can put some pace on your return. As a rough rule of thumb, your racquet should have reached the limit of its backswing as the server's ball crosses the net. At that point, you should be ready to move into your forward swing.

5. Track the ball

As you prepare to return serve, you must make a series of rapid decisions about the flight of the ball. Is it going to the right or left? Will it land deep or shallow in the service box? Will it bounce high or low? To make these decisions, you must watch the ball intently. Fix your eyes on it before it leaves the server's hand. Follow it as it rises to be hit by the racquet.

You can start to make some intelligent guesses about the serve even before the ball is hit. For example, most players will release the ball in the same place for a slice or flat serve, but for a twist serve the release is usually closer to the body. Then, of course, you must track the ball as it comes toward you. But start watching the ball the moment it leaves the server's hand.

6. Move in for slower serves

It's best to be on the baseline when you return serve. From that position, you will have time to react, prepare and hit the ball. However, if the server has a weak second serve, move in and take the ball early. The weaker serve will be slower so that you'll be putting a little extra pressure on the server, both on his delivery and on his preparation for your return since he'll have less time to get ready for it. And you'll be closer to the net so you can continue to move forward and be in a good position to hit a solid volley with your next shot.

Move up at least one full step farther into the court when you are receiving a second serve because it will probably be slower and land closer to the net. If the server is particularly weak, take two or three more steps toward the ball.

7. Hit through the ball

Don't try anything fancy when you return serve. Be content with a solidly hit shot that goes deep into your opponent's court or, in doubles especially, crosscourt to the feet of the oncoming server. Hit the ball as you do a normal ground stroke—firmly, about waist high and just ahead of your front foot. If the ball bounces high, adjust your swing to contact the ball higher. But if the ball bounces low, bend your knees so that you still make contact at about waist height.

Keep a firm wrist and grip, particularly on hard-hit first serves, as you make contact with the ball. A floppy wrist will produce erratic returns, especially on any off-center hits. A firm wrist will give you better direction and more pace on your returns.

Keep the racquet on the ball as long as possible by hitting through the ball in the direction you want the ball to go. Your racquet should first follow the ball's line of flight and then sweep into a full follow-through as it does on a conventional ground stroke. If you follow through completely, you'll increase your chances of hitting through the ball.

8. Keep moving after your return

As you improve, you should move to the center of your opponent's possibilities—that is, the middle of the path his shot could take and land in court. For example, if you return down the center of the court in singles, you should move to the center of your court. But if you hit short or down the line, your opponent's possible angle of return is larger.

Whatever you do, stay on your toes. As soon as you finish your follow-through, get moving to handle the server's next shot and move immediately to the center of your court. In singles, that's close to the center mark, just behind the base-line; in doubles, in the center of your half of the court, either up or back as the situation dictates.

Checklist for the return of serve

1. Watch the ball from the moment it leaves the server's hand.
2. The faster the serve, the shorter your backswing must be.
3. Turn your upper body and get your racquet back before the ball crosses the net, if possible.
4. Hit through the ball with a firm wrist and a full follow-through.
5. Hit your returns deep if the server stays back or low to the feet of a net-rushing server.

HOW TO HIT THE FOREHAND VOLLEY

No matter what the level of your play, an effective volley should be a part of your stroke repertoire. Crisp, well-controlled volleys are the keys to success at the net in both singles and doubles.

Some players are reluctant to go to the net because they cannot volley adequately. However, the volley is a simple stroke that many advanced players consider easier than the ground strokes. The volley has almost no backswing and a short, punching forward swing. So the shorter you can make your stroke, the easier the shot becomes.

On the other hand, when you play at the net, you will have less time to react to your opponent's shots, especially in doubles when all four players may be at the net. So your reactions must be faster and more instinctive.

To help you develop your volleys, we'll begin with a step-by-step description of the forehand volley and then take up the backhand volley as well as the more demanding high and low volleys.

1. Get set at the net

Net play demands alertness and anticipation—even more than is required at the baseline because the ball arrives more quickly. Your eyes must be glued to the ball and your body should be flexed, ready to move fast. Put your weight on the balls of your feet. Your knees should be bent, and so should your waist to keep your weight forward. Hold your racquet out in front of you with the head above your hand and well up above the level of the net where the ball will be hit. Cradle the throat of the racquet in your non-racquet hand to help draw the racquet back when the ball comes.

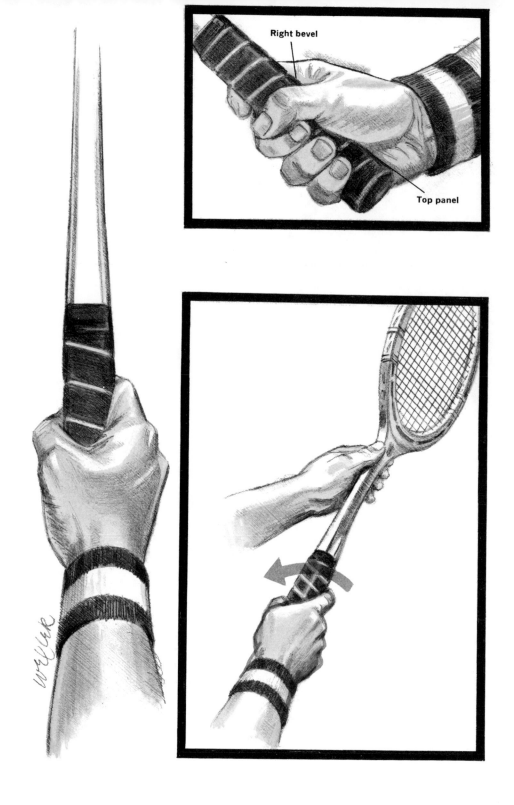

Right bevel

Top panel

2. Use one grip for all volleys

When you first begin to play the net, use your usual Eastern forehand and backhand grips for volleying. (Shake hands with the racquet for the Eastern forehand, rotate your hand one-quarter of a turn upward for the backhand.) But as your play improves, you'll find you won't have time to switch grips and still cope with the rapid-fire exchanges at the net. Then, find a grip—somewhere between your forehand and backhand grips—which will permit you to hit all volleys comfortably using only that grip. We recommend the Continental grip shown here. To get to the Continental from an Eastern forehand grip, rotate the racquet about an eighth of a turn so that the base of your thumb is on the top panel of the racquet handle (see top inset). Your thumb should be wrapped around the handle and the base knuckle of your forefinger should be on the right bevel of the handle (for a right-hander).

3. Pivot to get your racquet back

In the rat-a-tat-tat exchange of shots at the net, you'll rarely have time to turn your body, step to the ball and then hit—as you would with a ground stroke. You must, though, pivot your upper body to get your racquet back to a position even with your shoulders. If you rotate your shoulders as soon as you anticipate where your opponent's shot will go, your racquet will swing back automatically with very little arm motion. When you have time, step toward the ball, with your left foot if you're a right-hander. That way you'll be able to put extra power into the shot.

4. Squeeze the racquet

The action of hitting a volley is a blocking or punching motion with the head of the racquet held above the level of the gripping hand to give maximum leverage on the swing. That calls for a firm wrist and a tight grip on the racquet. If you hit your volleys with a loose grip, the racquet will wobble in your hand, causing you to lose control of the shot. So as you are about to hit the ball, squeeze your grip tighter and your wrist will firm up automatically. That will produce decisive volleys with accurate placement.

5. Hit out in front

Meet the ball out in front of your body to get the proper punching action. Hit the ball about six inches to a foot ahead of your front leg. Keep your racquet head up and tilt the racquet face back slightly. If you have your racquet face tilted forward, you'll hit down and into the net. The volley hit is a slightly downward punching motion almost like a slice. But don't tilt the racquet face too far back or the combination of the open face and the slicing action will make the ball go straight up in the air. Hit out and forward so the ball will go over the net and down into your opponent's court.

6. Watch the ball

When you're involved in some fast action at the net, it's vital to keep your eyes on the ball. You'll find it's easier to do that if you hit the ball out in front and get your body down so that your eyes are closer to the line of flight of the ball. If you let the fast-moving ball get past your front knee, you may lose sight of the ball and increase your chances of flubbing the shot. Hit out in front and you'll see the ball for a longer period before it hits the strings of your racquet.

7. Punch your follow-through

The volley follow-through is a jab rather than a roundhouse swing. You don't require a long follow-through as you do with a ground stroke because of the brief ball contact and the need for a rapid recovery. The finish of the volley follow-through should be a sharp, abbreviated punch in the direction that you're aiming the ball. Think of tying a string from the point of contact to the place you'd like the ball to go. Punch your follow-through along that line.

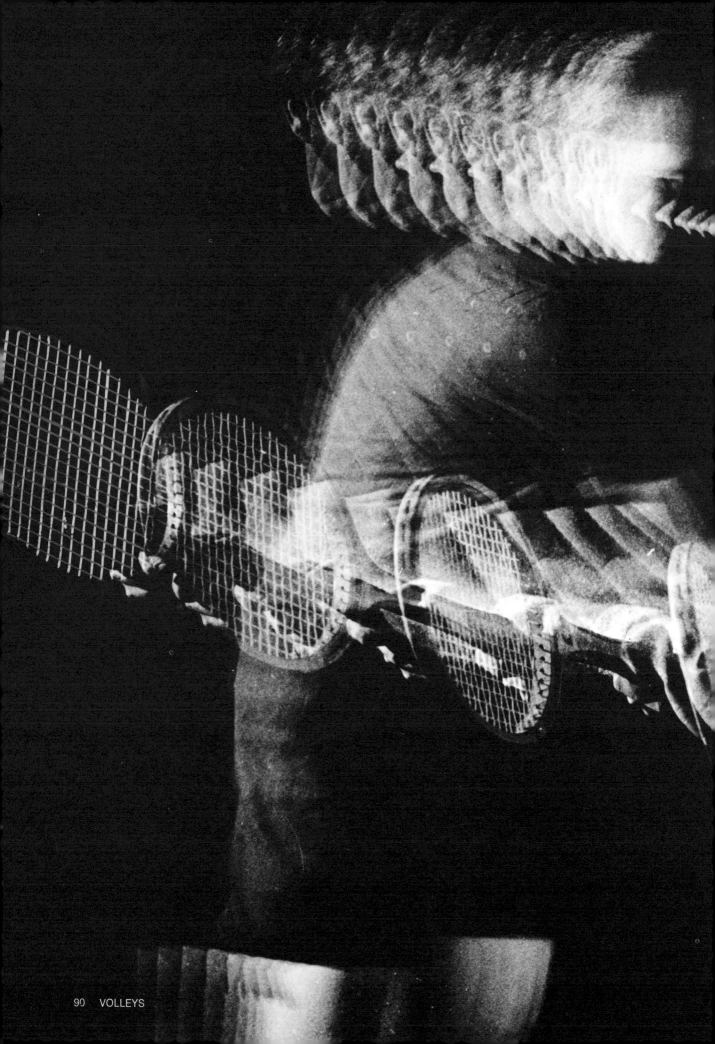

Checklist for the
forehand volley

This stroboscopic sequence photo of Ron
Holmberg hitting a forehand volley helps
underline the points to remember when you
execute the stroke:

1. Watch the ball.
2. Use a firm wrist and grip.
3. Hit the ball out in front.
4. Keep the racquet head up.
5. Use a short, punching stroke.

Keep this checklist in mind when you're
playing the net and your volleys will have the
crisp, controlled action you'll need for
winning shots.

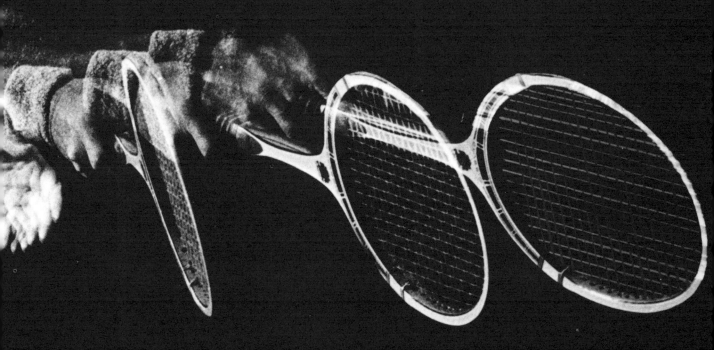

HOW TO HIT THE BACKHAND VOLLEY

Many average players regard the backhand volley as one of the more sophisticated shots in tennis. Actually, it's one of the simplest—because the swing is brief and uncomplicated, and because the ball is visible right out in front of the body throughout the stroke.

Most better players find the backhand volley easier than the forehand because the stroke is unrestricted by the player's body. However, an effective backhand volley must be hit out in front, which calls for fast reactions and quick preparation.

1. Use the other hand

Prepare for the volley by standing in a slight crouch with your weight on the balls of your feet. All players except beginners should use the Continental grip (reached by rotating the hand one-eighth of a turn upward from the standard Eastern "shake-hands" grip). Grasp the throat of the racquet lightly with the finger-tips of the other hand. When the ball approaches the backhand side, use this hand to draw the racquet back. That will help you position your body and racquet correctly for the stroke. But don't drag the racquet head back with the other hand; just guide it.

2. Pivot your shoulders first

The first movement from the ready position is to pivot your
shoulders so that your upper body will be parallel to the
expected line of flight of the ball. This motion will bring your
weight back and start your racquet on its short backswing. Stop
the racquet when it's by your rear shoulder and keep the
racquet head cocked above the hand. If you have time, step
into the shot for more power. But even on a hurried volley,
remember to get those shoulders around first. And watch
the ball.

3. Punch the ball

Bring the racquet forward to meet the ball with a short
punching motion in the direction you want the ball to go. Note
that on the forward swing the two arms move as if you were
stretching a long rubber band between them; the stroking arm
goes forward while the other one continues on back. Meet the
ball with your racquet out in front of your body and follow
through along the line of flight of the ball. But make it a brief
follow-through so you can recover and prepare for the next shot
which is apt to arrive soon when you're at the net.

4. Make contact out in front

It's vital on the backhand volley to hit the ball six inches to a foot out ahead of the body. That permits you to see the ball better and to get some power in the shot. At contact, have a firm wrist and a tight grip on the racquet so it won't wobble and produce a weak stroke. The racquet head should be held higher than your gripping hand to give maximum leverage on the shot.

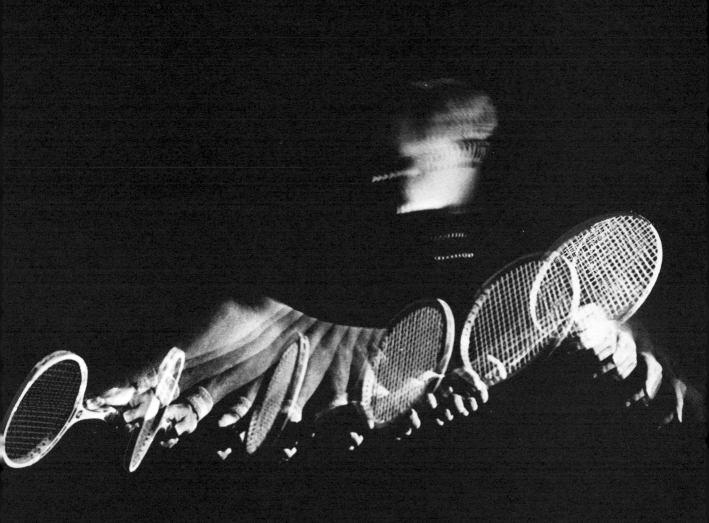

Checklist for the backhand volley

Study the stroboscopic action sequence of Ron Holmberg hitting a backhand volley for the essential points to remember on your own shots.

1. Watch the ball.
2. Use a firm wrist and grip.
3. Hit the ball out in front
4. Keep the racquet head up.
5. Use a short, punching stroke.

If you keep this checklist in mind for all your volleys, you'll soon develop the smooth action you need to win at the net.

HOW TO HIT DIFFICULT VOLLEYS

High Forehand

Get to high volleys fast

Balls that arrive high and wide—but not high enough to be smashed—must be volleyed out in front of the body. You can see the ball better there and put more strength in the shot. So don't let high volleys get too far before hitting them. Keep your wrist and grip firm for good stroke control.

High Backhand

Don't try to slice the ball; it isn't high enough for that. Meet it squarely and get your weight forward as you hit. Then, push toward the direction you want the ball to travel and use an abbreviated follow-through.

Low Forehand

Bend for low volleys

On low volleys, get your eyes down as close as you can to the line of flight of the ball. That not only helps you keep your eyes on the ball, it also forces you to get your body and racquet down for a smooth, controlled shot. If you don't bend but

Low Backhand

merely drop the racquet head to the level of the ball, you'll wind up scooping the ball with a weak, wristy motion. When you get down, hit the ball out in front of the body and follow through in the desired direction.

Block those balls hit straight at you

What do you do at the net when a ball comes straight at your body and you don't have time to step to one side for a conventional forehand or backhand volley? Place your racquet in front of you and hit a blocking backhand—or reflex—volley. There's no room for a backswing as such. But if you keep your wrist firm and straight, you can meet the ball squarely. That way, you'll be playing the ball —it won't be playing you. Lean forward to get your weight behind the shot. Then, try to aim it at a spot in the other court and follow through in that direction.

HOW TO HIT AN OVERHEAD

Many weekend players seem to have a fear of the overhead. And, indeed, the positioning and timing that are required make it a shot that's hard to hit well. But, if you take your time with the stroke, don't always go for the booming smash and, most importantly, practice the shot often, you can develop a reliable and accurate overhead.

The overhead is, of course, the normal reply to a lob by your opponent. If the lob is high, or if you lack real confidence in your overhead, it's best to let the ball bounce and hit it as it comes down for the second time. The ball will be moving more slowly and you'll have more time to get into position and prepare for your stroke.

Here, we'll review the fundamentals of hitting an overhead after it's bounced and then study the more advanced art of taking an overhead on the fly.

HOW TO HIT AN OVERHEAD ON THE BOUNCE

1. Skip to the shot

As soon as you see that your opponent has hit a defensive lob —in other words, one that travels high and deep into your backcourt —retreat as quickly as you can. Unless you have to run from close to the net to the baseline, it's best to turn your body sideways and skip or slide smartly backward until you are behind the point where the ball will fall after the bounce. Turning sideways will put your body in the hitting position and will help you start taking your racquet back. Get well back behind the ball. It's better to be too far behind and then have to slide forward than to be so close to the ball that you're forced to hit it leaning backward. Move back to hit an overhead the way a baseball outfielder moves back to take a fly ball. As the catch is made, the outfielder will be moving in to the ball. You should do the same.

2. Watch the ball

When your opponent hits a high lob, you should almost always let the ball bounce before attempting an overhead. You'll have more time to get ready for the shot and, then, too, there's always the chance that the ball may bounce out of court, ending the point in your favor. However, you must keep your eyes on the ball as it comes down, bounces up and then comes down for the second time. Ignore your opponent; his position is not really important. Remember, too, that the ball will be moving more slowly after the bounce, so that it's easier to time it.

3. Adjust your position

Many players move back rapidly to hit an overhead, but never seem to be in the right position when the ball finally arrives. That's because it's not enough merely to get behind the flight of the ball and its bounce. You must make small adjustments in your position until just before contact with the ball. That's especially important if you're playing outdoors where quite small puffs of wind can easily change the ball's flight. As you adjust your position, you should have your racquet back and, of course, you should be sideways to the direction you expect to hit the ball. Take the racquet back by lifting it up in front of you and dropping it behind your shoulder. Don't use the roundhouse swing of the serve.

4. Keep your elbow high

As you move back for a lob, you should be turning sideways and lifting your racquet. That way, all you'll have to do when you're set for the shot is drop the racquet head behind you to complete the backswing. You don't need to take the racquet back and down as far on the backswing as you do with a serve. But you must swing back far enough to get your elbow high and your forearm parallel to the ground before you start your forward swing. The combination of a high elbow and a dropped racquet head will force you to cock your wrist. Now, you'll be in the best position to unleash a powerful swing using your shoulder, arm and wrist to give maximum acceleration to the racquet head. Preparing to hit an overhead is like getting ready to throw a ball—take your arm back and keep your elbow up to start the snap.

5. Move into the shot

Position yourself behind the point where the ball will land. You will then have to slide forward as you begin your forward swing; this movement will put your body weight into the shot and, thus, add extra power. It is possible to hit an adequate smash with only shoulder rotation and wrist snap. But whenever you are able to, you should move into the shot just as you should transfer your weight forward with a serve. As you swing up to meet the ball, allow your shoulder to rotate. That will bring your back foot forward and thrust your weight into the shot.

6. Hit out in front

If you have moved back behind the ball, you'll have no difficulty in hitting the ball in front of you. But if you let the ball get behind you, you'll have a much more awkward shot to make and you'll lack power since you won't be able to put any weight into it. You'll also have to hook the ball down to make sure that you don't hit it too long. Aim for a contact point just ahead and slightly to the right of your body. If you were to let the ball fall without hitting it, it should strike the ground in front of your toes. Keep your head up and watch the ball through contact.

7. Snap your wrist

The key to hitting an overhead with power is to snap your wrist on the forward swing to accelerate the racquet head. Do it fast enough so that you would hear a definite "whoosh" if you were to try the shot without actually hitting the ball. As you start your forward swing, your wrist should be cocked (left). Uncock your wrist as your arm comes up by snapping your wrist through the contact with the ball (center) and into the follow-through (right). Make sure you have a firm grip; the wrist snap makes the racquet head travel faster than normal and a loose grip could produce a flubbed shot. At contact, your arm, wrist and racquet should be in a straight line and your body should be leaning forward slightly. Allow the wrist snap to continue after contact and then complete the follow-through on the opposite side of your body—just as you would for a serve. A good wrist snap calls for some strong arm muscles. If yours are not strong enough, build them up by squeezing an old tennis ball a dozen times or so whenever you have a spare minute.

8. Send the ball deep

Almost all overheads should be hit deep into your opponent's court. He or she will have great difficulty making any kind of return on an overhead that is hit with power and lands a couple of feet inside the baseline. If you can, hit your overhead away from your opponent to decrease the chances of any kind of return. However, a smash right to your opponent's feet can be just as effective. There's no need to telegraph the direction of your shot by turning your body. Keep your body sideways to the ball's flight. Then, a small adjustment of the wrist position will be enough to send your overhead sizzling into either corner.

Checklist for the overhead on the bounce

1. Watch the ball closely throughout the stroke.
2. Turn sideways to the net as you retreat.
3. Get your racquet back as you move into position.
4. Adjust your position continuously as you wait for the ball.
5. Stay behind the ball so that you make contact in front of your body.
6. Hit with maximum wrist snap.

HOW TO HIT AN OVERHEAD ON THE FLY

Hitting an overhead on the fly—that is, before the ball has bounced—is one of the hardest shots in the game for the average player. But there are times when you simply have no other choice. If your opponent sends up a high lob, then it will always pay you to let the ball land and bound up before hitting the overhead. But if the lob is relatively low, you'll have to take it in the air.

1. Turn sideways

As soon as your opponent hits a low, offensive lob—the kind you have to take out of the air—turn sideways to the net (photo A) and slide back swiftly to the point where you expect the ball to fall. That will put you in the proper position to start the overhead swing. It will also help you to take your racquet back early and get weight on your back foot so you can transfer it into the shot. As you turn sideways and retreat, you should be about a foot or so to the left of the ball's line of flight so that you can hit the ball above your right shoulder (for a right-hander) and not directly above your head.

2. Watch the ball

A beginning tennis player has to learn to watch the trajectory of a ball coming over the net and to make a quick estimate of where and how high the ball will go. On ground strokes, you have plenty of time to get into position and to make small adjustments as the ball approaches. On a low trajectory lob, though, there's little time to get into position and prepare. Thus, it's especially important to focus sharply on the ball. Some players like to use the other arm to sight the ball, as Trabert is doing in photo B, so that they can more easily adjust their position on the court as the ball approaches. Using your arm in this way will also help you keep your balance.

3. Use a compact backswing

Although the forward swing of an overhead is very much like that of a flat serve, the backswing should be much shorter. You don't have the time to bring the racquet down and up behind you as you do with the roundhouse swing of a serve. Take the racquet up in front of you as you turn sideways to prepare for the shot (photo A). Then, swing it over your shoulder (C) and drop the racquet head, which cocks your wrist (D). There's no need to take the racquet back into a deep backscratching position; but do remember to keep your elbow high so that you can swing the racquet head with the same kind of snap you use to throw a baseball.

4. Uncoil like a spring

To hit a powerful shot, your racquet head must be moving at maximum speed at impact with the ball. The forward swing starts with a rotation of the shoulders and a straightening of the arm as your forearm swings the racquet up (photo E). Then, as the racquet approaches the ball, you should uncock your wrist to begin the wrist snap (F) which will continue through contact and into the follow-through. The entire body action is like the uncoiling of a powerful spring. When you hit the ball on the fly, it's not easy to put your weight into the shot. But you can still hit a powerful overhead with a good shoulder rotation and a strong wrist snap.

5. Keep your feet on the ground

Unless you must jump to reach the ball, you should hit an overhead with your feet on the ground. As long as you stay in contact with the court, you can push off with your back foot to transfer your weight into the shot and, thus, hit a more powerful overhead. If there's time, slide back a couple of steps so that you'll be behind the ball as it comes down. That way, the ball will be low enough so that you will not have to jump and you'll be able to make contact in front of your body. Don't let the ball get too low, however, or you'll be hitting with a cramped arm action and, consequently, produce a weak shot. Make contact with your arm and upper body outstretched and with your body weight behind the shot. Your rear foot will move forward as you complete the shot, just as it would for a serve. But your front foot should remain in contact with the court.

6. Jump only when you must

You'll often see a professional tennis player leap into the air to take an overhead on the fly. That's because the ball would pass over the top of the racquet if the player did not gain that extra height by jumping. And in the fast exchanges of professional play, a player frequently has little time to retreat to get in the best position to hit an overhead. If you can, slide back and hit an overhead with your feet on the ground. If you don't have time, bend your knees as you turn sideways and then jump up as the ball comes close. How you jump is not important; the idea is to gain as much height as possible so you can reach the ball. It is important, though, that you hit the ball with a good wrist snap since you will not be able to put any weight into the shot. You can still hit a hard smash by pulling your upper body forward and snapping your wrist. But remember, if you have a choice, stay on the ground.

7. Finish your follow-through

The follow-through on an overhead should be just like that on a hard flat serve. Continue your wrist snap after contact with the ball (photos G and H) and allow your racquet to swing around your body so that it finishes up pointing toward the back fence (I). If you stop your follow-through too early, the chances are that the racquet will be decelerating as contact is made with the ball. A full follow-through, on the other hand, will insure that the racquet head is moving at top speed when you hit the ball. It will also help you transfer your weight forward as you stroke the ball. If you hit the ball well out in front, you'll have to bring your back foot forward to keep your balance.

Checklist for hitting an overhead on the fly

1. Watch the ball closely throughout the stroke.
2. Turn sideways as soon as you see a lob coming.
3. Prepare early and use a compact backswing.
4. When possible, keep your feet on the ground to put weight into the shot.
5. Contact the ball out in front of you with a strong wrist snap.
6. Use a full follow-through as you would on a serve.

HOW TO HIT A LOB

The lob is a stroke that many weekend players—because of a lack of
experience or skill or both—
neglect to use. That's a mistake.
Lobs are not hard to hit and they
can be effective weapons in many
situations on court.

The lob can be a defensive
stroke (the high shot depicted
below) used to get you out of a
tight spot. Or it can be an offensive
stroke (the lower shot) that's
intended to win the point outright.

The defensive lob is a high
arcing shot which usually loops
from baseline to baseline. It's
strictly a defensive shot, designed
not to win the point so much as it

is to give you time to get back into the game when your opponent has you on the run and out of position.

An offensive lob is usually hit when your opponent is close to the net and you're in a good position with the choice of going for a passing shot (a ball hit to the side of the opponent which he can't reach) or lobbing over his head. If it's hit correctly, the ball should drop deep in the backcourt so that your opponent does not have time to run back and retrieve it. This lob is always meant to be a winner.

First, we'll run through the essentials of the defensive lob and, next, those of the offensive lob.

Defensive Lob

Offensive Lob

HOW TO HIT A DEFENSIVE LOB

1. Prepare as you move

Chances are that you'll find yourself forced to use a defensive lob when you're scrambling just to get the ball back over the net and stay in the point. You probably won't have time to prepare properly for the shot as you do for a forehand or backhand drive. So get your racquet back as you run for the ball. Take a full backswing as though you are about to hit a drive and, if possible, turn your body sideways to the line of flight of the ball as you run. Don't attempt to disguise your swing—just get your racquet back so that you can take a full swing up through the ball.

2. Watch the ball

It's tough to concentrate on watching the ball when you are attempting to hit a defensive lob. That's partly because you will probably be scrambling as hard as you can and partly because your opponent will often have a good position at the net where it is tempting for you to keep half an eye on him. Ignore your opponent. Your problem is to get the ball back over the net and to stay in the point. You can do that only if you hit an effective lob and that means watching the ball all the way. You are going to hit the ball high in the air, and there's no opponent up there.

3. Take a full backswing
To hit a high and deep defensive lob requires a long flowing stroke with a full backswing and a complete follow-through. If you have already taken the racquet back as you're running for the ball, you'll be in a good position to hit a full stroke. Draw the racquet back until it's pointing toward the back fence or in the usual back-swing position you'd employ for a forehand drive. If you use a short backswing, you'll probably hit such a weak shot that the ball will merely pop up in the air, presenting your opponent with an easy putaway. Take a full backswing so you can make a complete forward swing.

4. Hit under the ball

A true defensive lob must go high in the air and, preferably, deep into your opponent's court. The height will give you time to recover and the depth will make it harder for your opponent to hit an effective overhead. So don't pussyfoot around. Get your racquet under the ball as you swing forward and loft the ball high into the air. Imagine that you are driving that ball up into the air. Send it high enough so that your opponent has plenty of time to look at it and think about it. Don't worry whether he'll have time to make a good return. Not many players can hit a good shot when the ball is falling almost vertically. Get under the ball and lob it high in the air.

5. Use a firm wrist

The defensive lob is not a tough shot involving a deft snap of the wrist. It's a drive that goes up in the air. Keep your wrist firm and your grip tight, just as you would with a normal ground stroke. Even though you may not have much time to make the shot, don't attempt to add something extra to the shot by flicking at the ball. Hit through the ball upward and outward by keeping your wrist firm throughout contact and into the follow-through. Remember, a defensive lob has to travel farther in the air than the full length of the court to be successful. So hit through the ball with a firm wrist and grip.

6. Aim down the center

It's not too difficult to hit a lob high in the air, but it can be difficult to hit a lob just hard enough so that it lands where it should: a couple of feet inside your opponent's baseline. And, of course, a lob is going to be affected by any wind. Thus, it pays to aim a defensive lob down the center of the court. If you go for one of the corners, the slightest error will probably send the ball out of court. No matter what your opponent's position is, hit your defensive lobs deep so that they land within a few feet of the distant baseline close to the center of the court.

7. Follow through high

The key to getting enough height on your lobs is the follow-through. Hit through the ball and follow through upward along the line of flight of the ball for as far as you can. The stroke should finish with the racquet high in front of you. If you aren't getting much height on your lobs, try exaggerating the follow-through to force yourself to hit through the ball and drive it in the air. The ball has to travel much farther in the air than a normal baseline-to-baseline ground stroke, so make your follow-through as full as if you were hitting a conventional ground stroke.

8. Get back into position

The major reason for using a defensive lob is to give yourself time to get back into a good position behind the center of the baseline so you can carry on with the point. Don't just stand around and admire your gracefully arcing lob. Use that time to get back into position and to prepare yourself for your opponent's reply to your lob. If you are facing an opponent with a good overhead, chances are he'll use it; so be on your toes, ready to move to either side. A defensive lob will give you breathing room. Take advantage of it.

Checklist for the defensive lob

1. Get your racquet back as you move for the shot.
2. Keep a firm wrist as you meet the ball.
3. Contact the ball from underneath and hit through it.
4. Watch the ball.
5. Follow through high and in the direction you wish the ball to go.
6. After you complete the shot, recover quickly to a good defensive position.

HOW TO HIT AN OFFENSIVE LOB

1. When to use it

The offensive lob is a surprise weapon that should be used discriminately and with as much disguise as possible. The best time to hit it is when your opponent is up at the net and you're set solidly on or inside the baseline. In that situation, the offensive lob is an alternative to a passing shot; instead of trying to smack the ball past your opponent, you hit it over him. Don't attempt an offensive lob if you're behind the baseline because your opponent will probably have time to back up and smash the ball on the fly. If you are close to the service line, a passing shot will be a higher percentage stroke.

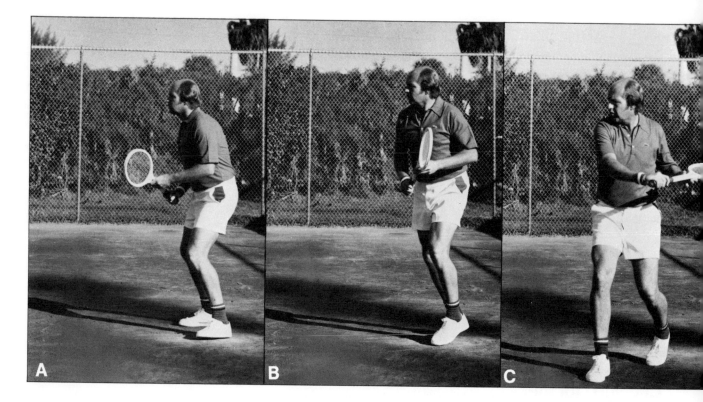

2. Disguise the shot

For an offensive lob to be successful, your opponent must have no inkling of what is about to happen until the ball leaves your racquet. Otherwise, he'll start backpedaling to get in position for it. So the preparation and forward swing for the stroke should be exactly the same as you would use for a forehand or backhand ground stroke. Remember, too, that although the offensive lob calls for a lot of touch, it is not a gentle stroke. You will have to hit through the ball. So take a normal backswing, just as you would for any other ground stroke. Make your decision to hit a lob before you start the stroke, but don't let your opponent know what's coming until you've hit the ball.

3. Watch the ball

For most weekend players, the offensive lob is not an easy shot. It calls for concentration and special care in contacting the ball. So you've got to keep your eyes glued to the ball. Forget about the opponent threatening you at the net. Concentrate on watching the ball before, during and after impact, and you'll hit a shot that has a good chance of being a winner.

4. Use a firm wrist

You've got to hit through the ball on the offensive lob to be sure it loops over and well beyond your opponent. That means you must keep a firm wrist throughout the stroke. If your wrist isn't firm, you'll hit a weak floater which can easily be picked off and smashed back by your opponent at the net. Use a firm grip and wrist, especially at contact and into the follow-through. Remember, you must hit the ball firmly so that it clears your opponent's racquet. But, of course, don't hit it so hard that it sails over the baseline.

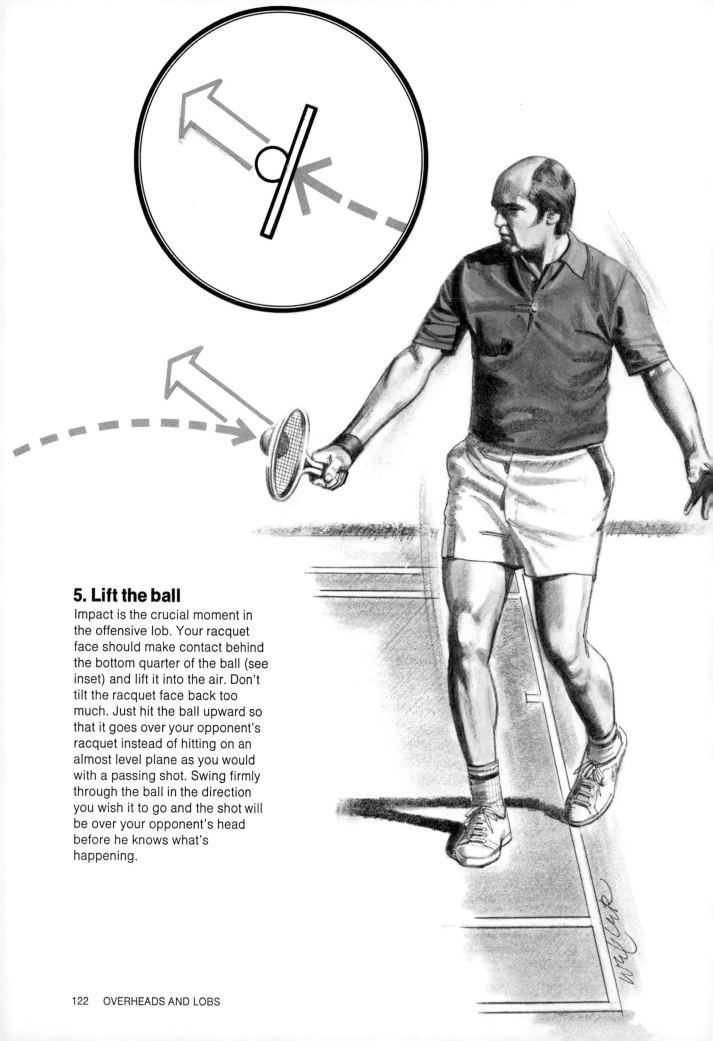

5. Lift the ball

Impact is the crucial moment in the offensive lob. Your racquet face should make contact behind the bottom quarter of the ball (see inset) and lift it into the air. Don't tilt the racquet face back too much. Just hit the ball upward so that it goes over your opponent's racquet instead of hitting on an almost level plane as you would with a passing shot. Swing firmly through the ball in the direction you wish it to go and the shot will be over your opponent's head before he knows what's happening.

6. Follow through fully

Follow through firmly as far as you can. Just after impact, your racquet should travel along the same path as the shot to make sure that you hit through the ball enough for it to clear your opponent's racquet. But don't stop your racquet there. Keep your follow-through going until the racquet finishes high in the air, pointing in the direction you wish the ball to go. When possible, aim your offensive lobs at your opponent's backhand side since that will give him a more difficult overhead to hit if the offensive lob doesn't quite work.

Checklist for the offensive lob

1. Always watch the ball.
2. Prepare as you would for a ground stroke.
3. Keep a firm wrist and grip.
4. Meet the bottom quarter of the ball and hit through it.
5. Follow through completely.

RAISE YOUR GAME WITH MORE ADVANCED STROKES

When you've developed a well-rounded game with a real command of the basic strokes and strategies of tennis, it's time to think about adding a few refinements and flourishes to your repertoire of shots. Advanced strokes—such as the approach shot, the drop shot, the topspin lob and the lob volley—will help elevate your game to a new level.

But be warned: these shots are not as simple as they often look. They take skill and work to hit under match conditions. And even then, your chances of success with them are less than with the fundamental strokes. They are low percentage shots to be used only when the situation is right and you're on top of your game.

Still, they're worth the effort involved in perfecting them. A deftly timed drop shot or topspin lob can not only startle an opponent and win you a tough point; the very knowledge that you possess such a shot can't help but unsettle him.

So as your game improves, try to augment it with some of these advanced strokes. Just remember that you should practice them a lot and employ them cautiously.

HOW TO HIT
AN APPROACH SHOT

The approach shot is a kind of hybrid stroke.
That is, it's not one particular, well-defined
shot like the backhand volley or the lob.
Rather, it is one of several possible strokes
you can use when you have one objective in
mind: to approach the net from the backcourt.
The approach shot, thus, is any stroke that you
hit between your baseline and service line
(above) as you charge up to a proper volleying
position near the net. But the approach shot
is best hit as a modified ground stroke.

Demonstrated by Roy Emerson

1. Shorten your backswing

Your chance to go to the net will come when your opponent
hits a short ball that bounces closer to the service line than the
baseline. When you realize that the ball will land short, start
your run into the court (frame A), taking your racquet back as
you do (A, B and C). Prepare as you would for a conventional
forehand or, as Roy Emerson demonstrates here, a backhand.

But there's no need for a full backswing since you won't have
to hit the ball the full distance of the court. In fact, accuracy
and consistency are more important than power with the
approach shot. Your goal should be to aim the ball deep toward
your opponent's weakness. You are trying to set up a situation
which will enable you to win the point with a volley when you
reach the net. So the approach shot will rarely be a winner. But
it should be a solid shot that your opponent will not be able to
return easily.

2. Keep it simple

The best stroke to use as an approach shot is one you hit well. If you normally hit a flat backhand or forehand, do just that on your approach. If you normally slice your ground strokes, then a little slice on the approach shot will help keep the ball low. Some top professional players can hit top-spin approach shots from almost anywhere on the court, but anything like that is probably too ambitious for the average player.

Keep it simple. Make sure you are turned sideways to the flight of the ball as it approaches. Pause momentarily so that you can transfer your weight into the shot, get down to the ball if you have to and hit through it with a smooth, controlled motion. There's a lot of pressure when you are trying to get to the net, so this is no time to try any low percentage shots. Simply use your best shot.

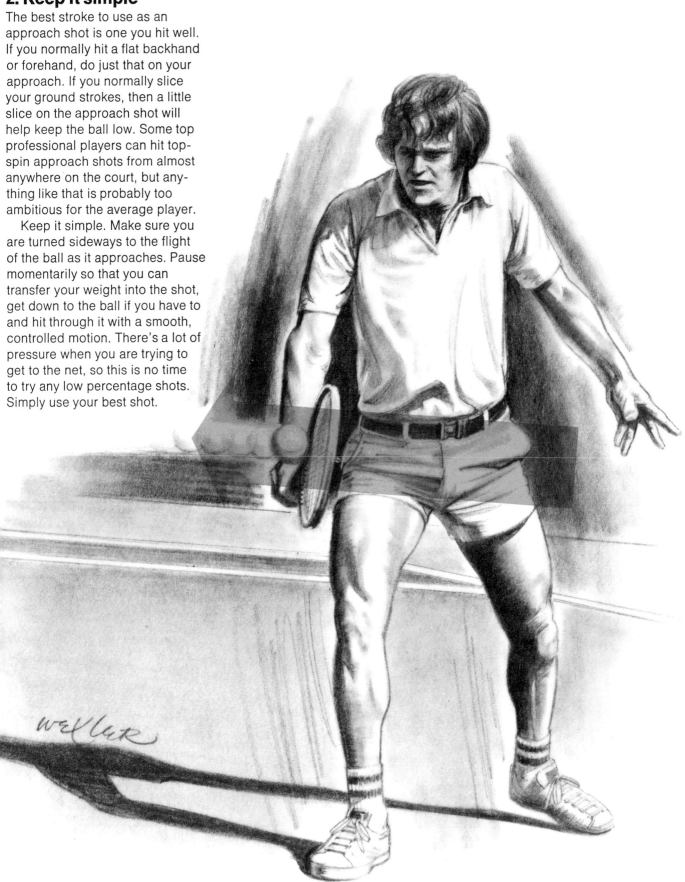

3. Follow through for direction

Placement is critical with the approach shot. If your opponent
is back on the baseline, you should hit the ball deep to his
weakness so that his return will present you with a relatively
easy chance to make a winning volley when you reach the net.
You should keep the ball on the racquet for as long as possible
(frame G) and follow through in the direction you wish the ball
to go (H, I). Use the full follow-through, as you would on a
normal ground stroke. But don't turn your body too soon or
you may pull the ball too sharply crosscourt. The racquet should
finish on the opposite side of your body (J) so that you are once
again facing the net and, of course, watching the departing
ball. Your weight should be moving forward; you can use that
momentum to keep going toward the net (K, L).

4 . Move to cover the angles

As you complete your approach shot, keep moving up to the ideal volleying position about midway between the service line and the net. If you hit your approach shot down the center of the court, your best volleying position will be straddling the center service line. But if you hit your approach shot deep to either corner, you should move slightly off center to cover your opponent's possible angles of return. For example, if you hit deep to your opponent's backhand corner (assuming that you are playing a right-hander) move to a position a little to the right of the center line. That way, you'll be at the midpoint of your opponent's target range and, as a result, be able to cut off a return with a minimum of movement.

Checklist for the approach shot

1. Keep your eyes on the ball, especially as you run up to meet it.
2. Get your racquet back quickly and use a shorter backswing than on normal ground strokes.
3. Take the ball as early as you can, preferably on the rise.
4. If the ball is low, stay down to make your shot.
5. Hit the ball deep to your opponent's weakness.

HOW TO HIT A DROP SHOT

The drop shot is a deceptively easy-looking stroke. But it isn't easy at all; actually, it's a difficult shot to hit with consistent accuracy.

You must appear to be about to hit a conventional ground stroke but then, at the last moment, slow your swing and gently brush the ball so that it drops over the net where it dies before your opponent can reach it (see below).

Done well, the drop shot is an effective shot that will often produce a winner. Done badly, it will plop into the net or sail too deep, giving your opponent a fine opportunity to ram the ball back past you for a winner. With the margin for error so small, you should attempt the drop shot only when your basic strokes are properly developed and you have confidence in your ability to control the ball. And even when you've mastered it, it is a surprise weapon to be used only occasionally.

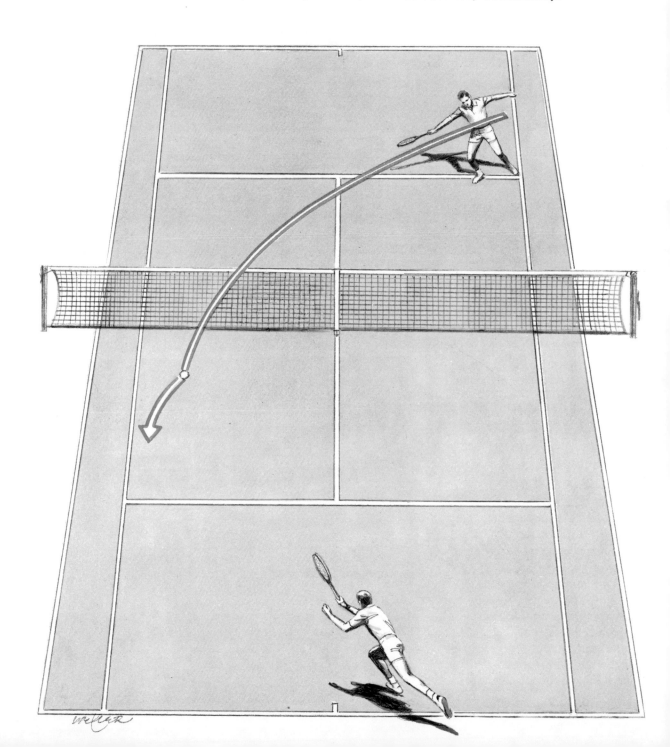

1. Pick your side

Although good players ought to be able to hit a drop shot from either the forehand or backhand sides, most develop a preference for one side. For example, Vic Seixas, shown in the photo sequence below, favors the backhand side for drop shots because he has a good underspin backhand. Underspin is what you want on a drop shot to take the speed off the ball. Thus, Seixas can disguise his drop shot by preparing for it the same way he prepares for his regular backhand. If you have a good underspin forehand, however, try the drop shot on that side. Although the forehand drop shot is not demonstrated in this book, the principles are the same.

2. Be in the right position

Don't try the drop shot unless you are in front of the baseline. You should be in an offensive position on the court where you have a choice of hitting a deep approach shot that will keep your opponent back and allow you to continue up to the net or a drop shot that falls just over the net where your opponent will not have enough time to run up and make an effective return. Don't attempt a drop shot from the baseline area. A drop shot travels relatively slowly and the distance it has to cover from the baseline should give your opponent time enough to run up and hit a return. So try it only when your opponent hits a ball which lands short—giving you the choice of hitting deep or going for the drop shot.

3. Prepare with deception

When you hit the drop shot, disguise it for as long as possible so that your opponent can't start coming in to return it. The backswing and forward swing should appear to be exactly the same as you use when you hit a sliced forehand or backhand. Take the racquet back early above the line of flight of the ball. Although you do not need a long backswing to hit a drop shot, you should give your opponent the impression that you are about to hit deep. Your preparation should be the same whether you are about to hit crosscourt or down the line. Remember that the drop shot is a surprise weapon. So keep your opponent guessing.

4. Move forward

When your opponent hits the kind of short ball that invites a
drop shot, you will probably have to move forward to take the
ball. Although the drop shot does not call for any power, step
into the shot as you would for any shot you intend to send deep
into the other court. That way, your opponent will think that you
are preparing to hit deep and will stay back behind the baseline. Bring the racquet forward and down as you step into the
shot with an open racquet face, and hit the ball gently.

5. Watch the ball

A drop shot demands far more touch than a ground stroke. So
even though a feel for the ball is perhaps the most important
factor in hitting a drop shot, it's no good having that feel if you
can't get the ball on your racquet. Thus, you must watch the
ball closely to help you hit it in the center of your racquet
strings. If you can actually see the impact, so much the better.
In any case, you should have a mental image of the ball hitting
your racquet. You can do that by concentrating on the
approaching ball.

6. Caress the ball

The key to hitting a drop shot is to take the pace off the ball so that it doesn't pop off your racquet and fly either too high or too far into your opponent's court. As you are about to meet the ball, open your racquet face slightly to caress the back and the bottom of the ball (inset). It's almost as though you are trying to catch the ball on your racquet. As you make contact, the racquet head should be moving on a downward and forward path so you automatically put some underspin on the ball. That will help you control the ball and reduce the forward bounce when it drops in your opponent's court. Be sure to follow through in the direction you want the ball to go. If you can hit a good slice serve, then you already have a feel for the movement of the racquet head around the side of the ball. See if you can translate that into the gentler, caressing action of the drop shot around the back and under the ball.

7. Get ready for the return

Since the drop shot is a relatively low percentage stroke, you cannot afford simply to stand and admire your handiwork. If you hit the ball a little harder or longer than you had intended, your opponent will have time to run up and hit a good return. In fact, many experienced players answer a drop shot with another drop shot. So you should be ready either to move in closer to the net or to recover quickly for a deeper shot. Of course, if you have hit a good drop shot with lots of deception, your opponent will not get to the ball in time and you'll win the point.

Checklist for the drop shot

1. Watch the ball.
2. Hit the drop shot only from in front of the baseline.
3. Prepare as you would for an underspin ground stroke.
4. Caress the ball to take the pace off it.
5. Follow through in the direction you wish the ball to go.
6. Recover quickly after you've hit the ball.

HOW TO HIT THE HALF VOLLEY

Few players ever really want to hit a half volley. It's a difficult and subtle stroke—usually hit when you're in the no man's land between the service line and the baseline, and your opponent sends you a ball that lands at your feet.

Ideally, you'd probably prefer to take that kind of ball either early as a proper volley or late as a ground stroke. Instead, you have to hit the ball close to the ground, just after it's bounced, with a stroke that's neither a volley nor ground stroke; ergo, the half volley.

A   B   C

1. When you must half-volley

Essentially, the half volley is a shot that your opponent imposes on you. You are on your way up to the net, perhaps after serving, but when your opponent's shot arrives you are not near enough to the net to permit you to volley it comfortably. When you realize that, pause and get ready to hit a half volley.

The half volley is just about equally difficult off either the forehand or backhand. But you'll probably feel more comfortable hitting a half volley on the forehand side, as Roy Emerson demonstrates here and on the following pages.

Either way, the half volley calls for a little extra concentration on your timing so that you don't hit the ball late. So watch it carefully. Pause early enough so that the ball will bounce in front of you and you can make contact just in front of your forward knee. That way, you'll be able to see the ball better and keep it on the racquet longer.

D   E   F

2. Turn your body sideways

As soon as you decide that the shot is going to be a half volley, start turning your upper body so that your shoulders are almost parallel with the line of flight of the oncoming ball. This upper body rotation will help you accomplish several things. First, you will automatically start taking your racquet back. Although the half volley doesn't call for the long backswing of a conventional ground stroke, you don't have much time to prepare. So get your racquet back early. Secondly, your upper body rotation will help put your weight on your back foot so that you will move forward as you hit the ball, thus adding a little pace to the shot. And, thirdly, you'll find it easier to get down to the ball—as you must for a half volley—if you are turned sideways to the line of flight of the ball.

3. Get down for the shot

A true half volley must be hit with the racquet close to the ground so that you can make contact immediately after the ball bounces. That means you must get down to the ball both by flexing your body and by bending your knees. Start to bend your knees as you take your racquet back and stay down as you swing forward. Note that Emerson bends to the point that his rear knee is almost scraping the ground. You may hear those knee joints creak the first time you do it, but it's the only way to get down low.

You should be down low enough so that your racquet handle is practically parallel to the ground as your racquet approaches the ball. If you fail to get down far enough, then your racquet head will be much lower than your hand and you'll scoop the ball up instead of hitting it back low over the net. A scooped ball will sail invitingly over the net and give your opponent a perfect setup for ramming the ball back down your throat.

4. Keep the ball on your racquet

Hit the half volley with a firm wrist and with your racquet face almost at a right angle to the ground. You should try to make contact just in front of your forward foot. Bring the racquet forward with a slight upward motion (the ball has to rise to go over the net, remember) and carry the ball on your racquet for as long as possible. The longer you can keep the ball on the racquet strings, the more control you'll have. Don't try to hit a half volley hard; just stroke it firmly with a controlled swing. The ball should go relatively low over the net if your opponent is rushing in for the volley.

Think of your racquet as a basket that you are bringing up behind the ball. You are trying to catch the ball in the basket and then send it on its way over the net with a firm thrust, not a scooping action. You should also resist the temptation to slice your half volleys. A sliced ball will just pop weakly off your racquet and may not even go over the net.

5. Lift the ball over the net

Stay down as you hit the ball and let your racquet continue out in front of you on a slight upward plane. The slight upward motion of the racquet, together with an almost vertical racquet face, will be enough to lift the ball over the net. If you tilt the face of the racquet back too much or if you raise your body as you hit the ball, then the ball will go too high over the net and present your opponent with an opportunity for a putaway shot.

Although the swing for a half volley has to be more abbreviated than the one used for a ground stroke, there's no reason to shorten the follow-through. In fact, to make sure that you are hitting through the ball for as long as possible, your follow-through should be as complete as you can make it from the low half volley position.

Checklist for the half volley

1. Watch the ball.
2. Take a relatively short back-swing.
3. Get down to the ball and stay down through the shot.
4. Keep your racquet face almost flat to the ball at contact.
5. Complete your follow-through.

PUT VERSATILITY IN YOUR GAME WITH DROP AND LOB VOLLEYS

If you're a sound net player and are confident of your ability to hit conventional volleys well, it may be time to think of adding a new dimension to your game by learning the drop and lob volleys. These aren't easy shots, though. You must be a fairly accomplished player with good racquet control to bring them off consistently. But they will give you a dandy weapon with which to surprise opponents, and often win points outright, when used sparingly.

The drop volley is the net player's version of the drop shot hit before the ball bounces. It's employed when your

DROP VOLLEY

opponent, or an opposing doubles team, is back on the base-line. Hit properly, the drop volley will fall rapidly once the ball crosses the net and then bounce gently twice or more before your opponent can reach it.

The lob volley, on the other hand, is used when your opponent is crowding the net. It's an offensive shot hit high enough to clear the racquet of the opponent and, preferably, deep enough so that it is difficult to chase down and return.

LOB VOLLEY

HOW TO HIT A DROP VOLLEY

Disguise the shot

Hitting a drop volley is similar to hitting a normal drop shot. But disguise the shot so it looks like a regular underspin volley, then take enough speed off the ball so it drops rapidly after crossing the net.

So prepare for the shot (frames A and B) with the same kind of short backswing you'd use for an underspin volley. As the ball approaches (C and D), reach out and meet it well in front of the body (E). Try to catch it on the strings (see opposite page) and push it back over the net (F). Then, stop the racquet so that there is almost no follow-through (G, H).

A B

C D E

F G H

Demonstrated by Bill Price

144   ADVANCED STROKES

Catch the ball

A drop volley demands real "touch." You've got to absorb the speed of the oncoming ball, then return it so that it falls just over the net—and doesn't go into it or land so deep in the other court that your opponent can race up and blast the ball past you.

The secret is to try to catch the ball on the face of your racquet. The face should come under the ball slightly (see inset) with just enough forward movement to give the ball sufficient momentum to clear the net. It should be pushed, gently but firmly, in that direction.

The most common error on the drop volley is to take too big a swing at the ball. Try to use almost no stroke at all—with a brief backswing and a very abbreviated follow-through—and you'll soon get the feel of the drop volley.

Checklist for the drop volley

1. Disguise your stroke by preparing as for an underspin volley.
2. Take the speed off the ball by catching it on your racquet.
3. Push the ball gently but firmly to clear the net.
4. Use a very short follow-through.

HOW TO HIT A LOB VOLLEY

Hit off low balls

The lob volley is a shot to use occasionally when both you and your opponent are up at the net and you have to retrieve a relatively low ball. (Never try a lob volley when you can meet the ball above net level.)

Prepare for a lob volley as you would for a normal low volley (frames A and B). Meet the ball out in front (C and D) and lift it firmly in the air (D and E). Follow through in the direction you wish the ball to go (F, G and H). A long follow-through isn't necessary, but you should recover quickly in case your opponent manages to make a return.

Lift the ball quickly

Hit a lob volley no harder than you would a conventional volley. If you strike the ball too hard, it will probably sail over the baseline. If you hit it too gently, it will present your opponent with a setup he can smash back down your throat.

Try to lift the ball quickly in the air by tilting the racquet face back at contact (see inset) and moving it on a rising plane into a moderate follow-through. That way, you'll be sure of hitting through the ball with control rather than merely popping the ball off the racquet and hoping your opponent won't be able to reach it.

Checklist for the lob volley

1. Don't use the lob volley if you can hit down on the ball.
2. Prepare as you would for a normal low volley with a short backswing.
3. Open the racquet face as you hit and lift the ball quickly in the air.
4. Follow through in the direction you wish the ball to go.

HOW TO HIT A TOPSPIN LOB

A tennis player who masters the top-spin lob possesses that supreme weapon on court: a shot that is almost guaranteed to be a winner when it's hit right. The ball sails over the outstretched racquet of an opponent at the net and, because of its forward spin, it drops rapidly in the backcourt and bounces sharply away toward the back fence.

The topspin lob, though, is not an easy stroke to learn. It takes lots of practice to develop to the point where it can be depended upon in a match.

1. When to use it

The topspin lob is a shot which, like the offensive lob (page 120), should be used when your opponent is crowding the net and you're in a good position at the baseline. It's an alternative to a passing shot—a ball hit out of reach to the side of your opponent. You should be on or in front of the baseline. If you are too far behind the baseline, the chances of hitting a successful topspin lob will be reduced because your opponent at the net will have more time to react and backpedal to attempt a smash. If you are close to the service line, on the other hand, you're probably better off attempting a passing shot. You'll need to hit only one or two good topspin lobs in a match in order to convince an aggressive opponent to think twice about coming to the net.

2. Take a full swing

The unique feature of the topspin lob is the whirling forward rotation on the ball which sends it skittering away from the baseline after it has bounced. To put that kind of heavy topspin on the ball, you've got to use a pronounced looping swing which comes up under the line of flight of the ball. The racquet head should then move very rapidly upward as contact is made. Unlike the offensive lob, which is a disguised shot employing a considerable degree of touch, the topspin lob requires a violent swing at the ball. The harder you swing, the more topspin you'll put on the ball—provided that you brush firmly up the back of the ball. Don't try this shot on your backhand unless you have a strong topspin backhand ground stroke. The reason: it's unlikely you'll be able to swing hard enough on the backhand side.

3. Hit out front

At contact, you'll have to snap your wrist to put maximum forward spin on the ball. You can do that only if you hit the ball well out in front of your forward hip. If you hit the ball late, you'll be unable to snap your wrist and the shot will lack both spin and forward speed. Some top professionals are able to hit a topspin lob far out in front because they use a modified Western grip with the palm of the hand under the racquet handle.

Don't pussyfoot around with a topspin lob; really take a cut at it. If you merely flick at the ball and don't put some forward motion on your racquet, the ball will go up in the air—topspinning madly—but it may not have enough momentum to carry it over the head of your opponent. In that case, he'll crash it back down at you. Imagine that you are using a long, sharp knife to pare a thick slice off the back and top of the ball when you hit it. Take the fuzz off the ball as you brush up and over it.

4. Finish high

After contact, let the racquet continue on up and around your body. The racquet should end up high in the air so that you are looking at the departing ball over the upper part of your racquet arm. Don't stop the racquet after you've snapped your wrist at the ball. If you do that, the chances are your racquet head hasn't been moving at top speed as contact was made with the ball. And the result will be that you won't put enough topspin on the shot. You can let the racquet follow through easily since, if you've hit the topspin lob correctly, you won't have to worry about recovering for your opponent's return.

Checklist for the topspin lob
1. Watch the ball.
2. Take a looping swing and drop your racquet head below the level of the flight of the ball.
3. Make contact out in front of your forward hip.
4. Snap your wrist as you hit up and over the ball.
5. Follow through fully.

HOW TO HIT A BACKHAND OVERHEAD

The backhand overhead is an emergency stroke—a shot you should use only when you have no other choice. In most cases, when your opponent lofts a lob to your backhand side, you have time to move over to get under the ball and hit a conventional forehand overhead (see pages 106-111).

But there are occasions when your opponent catches you by surprise with a quick low lob that forces you to resort to a backhand overhead. Here's the way to hit it.

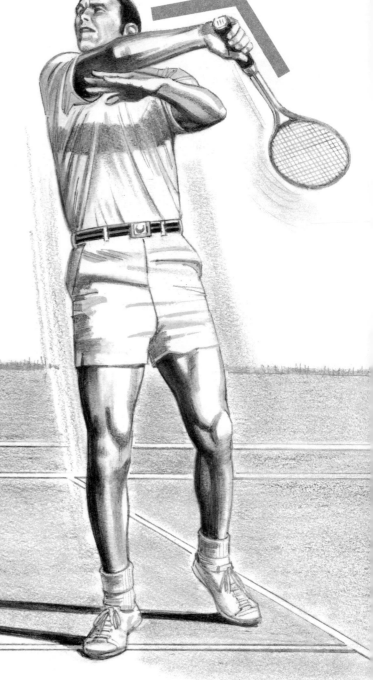

1. Turn sideways quickly

Since the backhand overhead is almost a desperation shot, you have to move fast to get into the well-balanced preparatory position that Vic Seixas demonstrates in the photos below. Turn sideways to the net as quickly as you can. Then take your racquet back with your hand in a high position and your racquet head dropped back. If the ball is about to pass over you, coil your upper body around until your back is almost facing the net. That way, you'll be further back and will have more of a chance to hit the ball in front of you.

2. Lay your wrist back

The preparation for a backhand overhead is more restricted than it is with the forehand version of the stroke because you can't get your arm back as far. Your chest interrupts the backswing. To compensate, you should lay back your wrist (photo C) before starting the forward swing. Draw your racquet back until its head is below the level of your hand. If your wrist is flexible, you will be able to get the racquet back further, as Seixas is doing here. By laying back your wrist on the backswing, you'll be able to snap the racquet forward sharply as you make contact. That's important since it's hard to put much weight into a backhand overhead. You must depend on that snap for almost all of the power in this shot.

3. Snap your wrist

It's tough to hit a backhand over-head with much power because you don't have enough time to get set and transfer your body weight into the shot. So you'll have to depend on your wrist snap and forearm motion for power. If you've laid back your wrist during the backswing, you'll be able to release that snap before and during contact. Your forearm should be straight at the point of contact and your grip should be firm. Keep the racquet head high through contact and resist the temptation to pull the ball down sharply. Go for depth with this shot to keep your opponent away from the net.

4. Stay up on the follow-through

Don't bring the racquet down sharply as you follow through. Keep the racquet head up as long as possible to be sure you hit through the ball. That way your shot will go deep and so be more difficult for your opponent to return. Follow through out in front of you as far as you can and then let the racquet come around naturally until you are almost facing the net. Keep the racquet head up and your arm straight until you complete your follow-through.

Checklist for the backhand overhead

1. Watch the ball.
2. Turn your body sideways to start the backswing.
3. Take the racquet back high.
4. Lay your wrist back before starting the forward swing.
5. Snap your wrist as you make contact with the ball.
6. Keep your racquet head up on the follow-through.

A

B

HOW TO PLAY AN ATTACKING GAME

Tennis singles is a demanding game, physically and mentally. To succeed at it, a player must have a repertoire of competent strokes, sufficient stamina to prevail in a long, tense match and a command of strategy which differs considerably from that involved in doubles.

In the first part of this chapter, we'll show you the basics of the attacking game in which the server usually charges the net and attempts to close out the point quickly with a well-placed volley. Following that, we'll concentrate on a more defensive approach to singles play —the backcourt game.

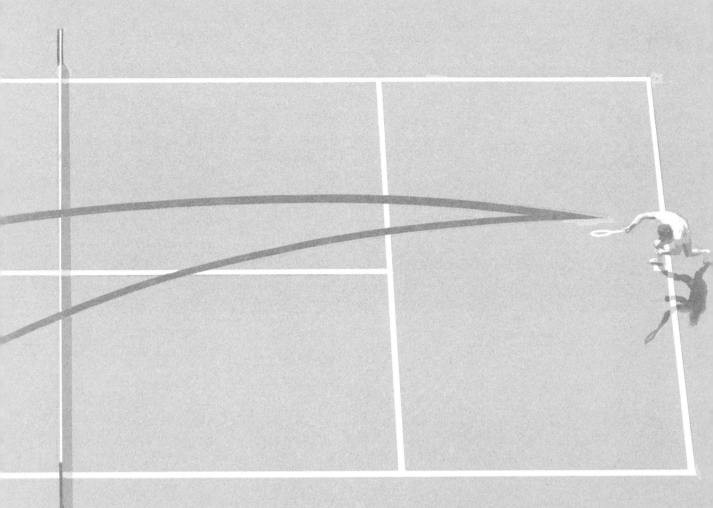

1. Be ready to charge the net

The foundation of the attacking game in singles is to be prepared to follow your first serve to the net so you can win the point on either your first or second volley. Start out by standing close to the center mark when you serve so you'll have the shortest distance to run to hit your first volley. Use a serve that you can hit deep and, in general, aim for your opponent's weakness if you're aware of it; for most players, of course, that will be the backhand.

Unless you are ahead in a match, it's best not to risk going for an ace. Instead, hit your first serve at about three-quarters of your maximum speed with enough spin to bring the ball safely down in the court. If you're serving to the deuce court, as shown here, your best bet is to hit down the center (A) to your opponent's backhand (if you're playing a right-hander). The chances are that your opponent will have difficulty returning with a backhand and you'll have less of an angle to cover (see next page) as you run up to take the return. Most players will hit a backhand return down the line, so you should be prepared for a backhand volley (if you are right-handed).

However, don't aim your serves to the same area all the time. If you do, your opponent will soon wise up and will edge over to prepare early for the return. Vary things a bit from time to time by serving wide to the side of the service box (B). That will pull the receiver out of court where he may be able to hit only a weak, floating return that can be volleyed easily. And, of course, he'll have to scramble back into position to take the next shot. If the receiver goes wide and returns down the line, then you'll have an opportunity for an easy backhand putaway volley.

Decide you're going to follow your first serve to the net before you deliver it. If you hold back waiting to see the ball bounce in the service box, you'll be too late to run up and volley your opponent's return. If you should try, the ball is likely to be returned to your feet and you'll have problems simply staying in the point. If you remember to release the ball well in front of your body, you'll automatically move into the court after you serve and be ready for a fast approach toward the net.

When your first serve is a fault, your second serve should be a relatively slower spin serve to avoid the possibility of a double fault. A good player should be able to follow a second serve to the net—especially on a fast surface. But the average player should stay back and wait for a short ball which will allow him to advance toward the net.

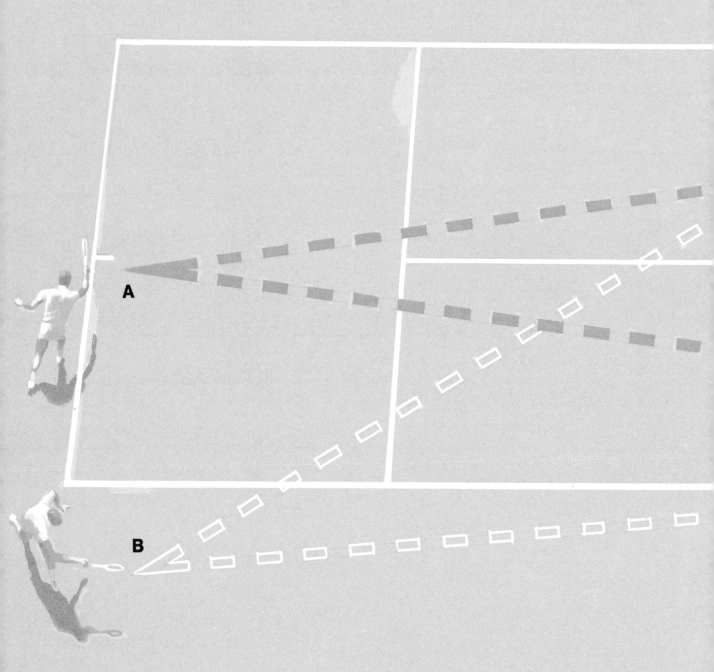

2. Cover the angles

In approaching the net after you serve, you should be a few feet behind the service line when the receiver hits the ball. Pause momentarily to determine the direction of the return and then move forward again toward the ball to hit your first volley. Where you move to depends on the placement of your serve and the angle of the receiver's return.

If you have served down the center into the deuce court (to point A), the chances are that the receiver will hit the ball down the line to your left. In that case, you can simply continue toward the net, and probably hit your first

volley with a backhand from around the "T" of the service boxes. Even if the receiver manages to put a little angle on the ball (his range of possibilities is defined by the dotted lines), a step to one side or the other should be all that's necessary for you to reach the ball and volley it effectively.

If, on the other hand, you've served wide to the receiver's forehand (point B), he has a wider choice of angle in making his return. Of course, that's somewhat offset by the fact that a wide serve is usually harder to hit for the average player. So the return is not likely to be hit powerfully. Still, you should be prepared to

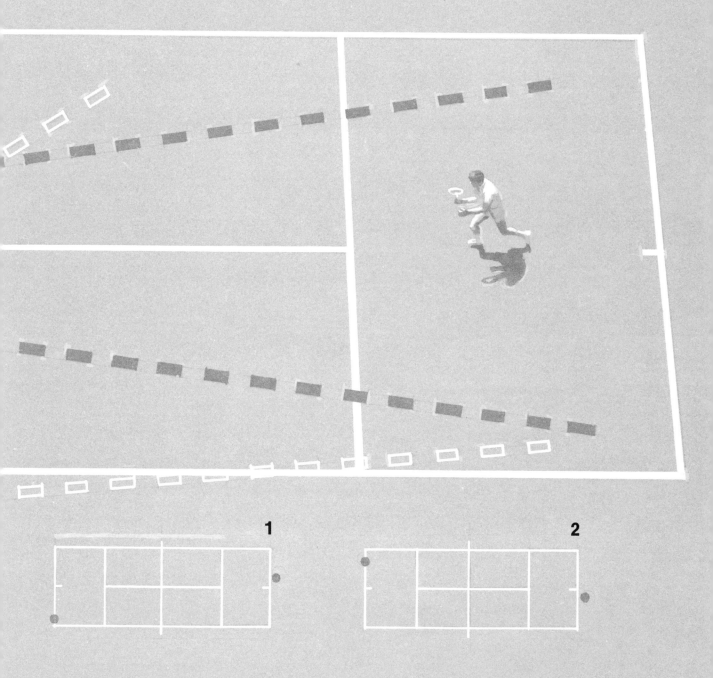

1

2

move more laterally than if you had served down the center. It's likely, though, that the receiver will return crosscourt to your right since that is the safer shot—the net is lower at the center and he has more court at which to aim. So you should prepare yourself especially for that kind of return. But beware: a good player may attempt a risky return down the line, probably into the corner, which will be hard for you to reach.

If you are receiving serve in singles on a fast court, you should position yourself so that you can handle either a down-the-center or a wide serve. In the deuce (or right-hand) court, that means with your right foot close to the singles sideline (see inset 1). In the ad court, you can afford to stand a little farther away from the singles sideline (see inset 2) since a right-handed server will not be able to pull the serve as wide in the ad court. On a slower court, you can afford to stand nearer the center. Watch the server closely and make your move as soon as you can see where the ball is going. On the first serve, concentrate on hitting the ball solidly and getting it back safely over the net. On a second serve, you can occasionally afford to run around your backhand and try for an outright winner.

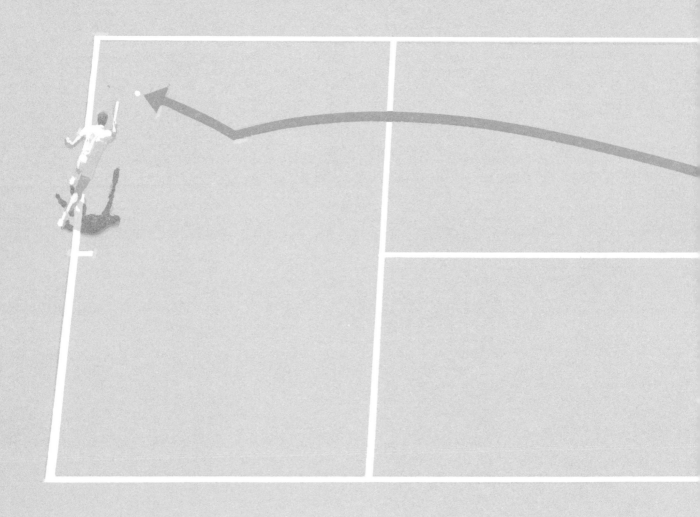

3. Hit your first volley deep

When you approach the net after serving, it's unlikely you'll be able to win the point with your first volley—unless your opponent hits a feeble return which sails high above the net so that you can hit down for an easy winner. You should, thus, concentrate on hitting a firm volley which goes deep into the other court, preferably to your opponent's weakness. Your objective should be to keep your opponent back at the baseline and to force him to hit up so you can continue to run up closer to the net and win the point by putting the second volley away.

Ideally, you should run up at least as far as the service line to hit your first volley. If you dawdle in following your serve, the ball will be dropping into your court by the time it reaches you, which will force you either to volley up or hit a half volley just after the ball bounces (see inset). It's hard to hit a good return with either of those shots. The closer you can get to the net, the higher the ball will be as you hit your volley. If you can meet the volley about chest high, then you should be able to make an aggressive shot which will probably go deep and keep your opponent back on the baseline.

Don't make the mistake of hitting your first volley too short. That will allow your opponent to come in and hit a passing shot

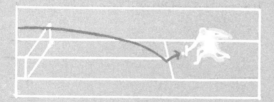

to your side that you may not even be able to touch with your racquet. If you've pulled the receiver out of court with your serve, hit your first volley into the empty half of the court so that your opponent has to hit an awkward shot on the run. You may even force an error and win the point. If your opponent is in a good center court position, volley the ball so that it lands as deep as possible in the hope of forcing him to hit up. A ball that is rising as it crosses the net can easily be volleyed down for a winner.

Don't stand there admiring your first volley. As soon as you've hit the ball, continue to move toward the net. By the time you are ready to hit your second volley, you should be in a commanding position about halfway between the service line and the net. Now, you'll be all set to make a winning shot.

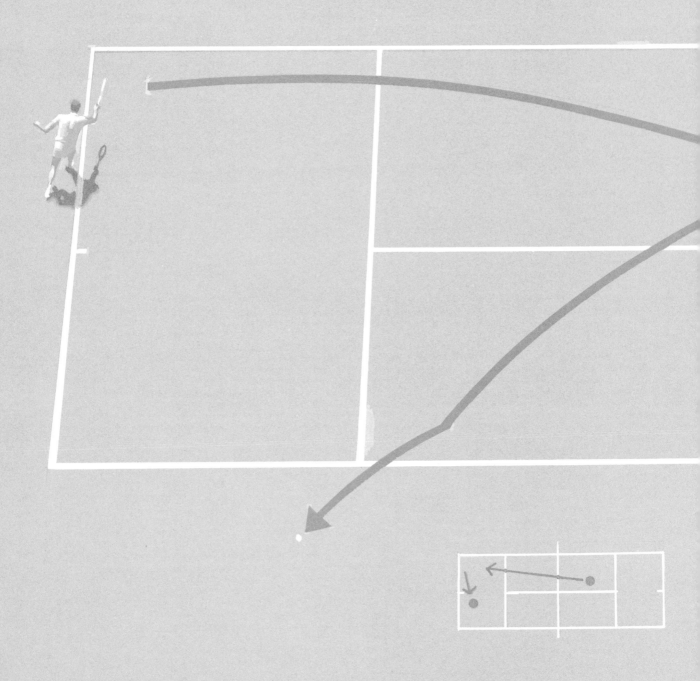

4. Put the ball away quickly

Singles is a game in which you sometimes have to take a risk. It is often better to take a chance on finishing a point rather than giving your opponent another chance to hit the ball. So your aim when you're on the attack in singles should be to take the net aggressively and to close out the point as quickly as possible.

If you can reach an ideal volleying position about halfway between the net and the service line, you ought to be able to put away any ball that is rising as it crosses the net. Hit a firm volley into the open space away from your opponent. If you have the chance to angle the volley sharply—as shown here—so much the better. However, don't angle the volley so sharply that you run the risk of hitting it out.

Occasionally, you will run up against an opponent who can anticipate your actions and return intended putaway volleys. When you encounter such a player, hit behind him. In other words, instead of hitting into the large open area (the deuce, or lower, court in the drawing above), hit to the smaller area on the other side. The chances are that your opponen

will already have begun to run across the court and you'll probably catch him wrong-footed (see inset). Once a player begins to move, it's tough to change direction even for a ball that comes relatively close.

But no matter where you decide to play your volley, make up your mind about it before you hit the ball and don't try something else at the last moment because of your opponent's movements. To put the ball away, you must hit the volley decisively so that your opponent cannot even get a racquet on the ball to make a return.

Checklist for an attacking strategy in singles

1. Get your first serve in and vary the spin and placement.
2. Play the percentages by using your most reliable shots.
3. When rushing the net, pause momentarily to determine the direction of your opponent's shot.
4. Hit your volleys deep unless you can put the ball away with an angled volley.
5. Whenever you hit the ball, start moving toward the center of the possible angles of return.

HOW TO PLAY A DEFENSIVE GAME

Most club players don't have the stamina and, very often, the aggressiveness necessary to play successful serve-and-volley tennis— charging the net behind their serves to try to overwhelm the opposition with quick, putaway volleys. They prefer to remain in the backcourt which is, indeed, usually the prudent course for all players after a weak second serve or on a very slow court.

On the following pages, you'll find the strategies you can use to develop a winning game by starting out in the backcourt in singles. If you're lucky, or good, you may be able to beat an opponent by remaining in the backcourt and forcing errors from him in the duel of ground strokes. But you'll increase your chances of winning considerably by advancing to the net when the right opportunity comes.

So most of the strategies here are designed to help you eventually take command of the net after you begin the point in the backcourt. The idea is to use both backcourt and net-rushing strategies as the situation and the opponent demand. Be like a lion in the grass; wait for your opening in the backcourt and when it comes, pounce.

1. Move your opponent around

When you stay back after serving or returning serve, your aim should be to keep your opponent on or behind the baseline. That way, there's less chance that your opponent will be able to hit a winning shot. In fact, there's a good chance he will lose his patience in a long baseline-to-baseline rally, go for a winner and, thus, commit an error.

So the first key to backcourt play is to hit the ball deep. All your shots should land closer to the baseline than to the service line. If you hit a short ball around the service line, your opponent will be able to come up, hit an approach shot and then continue toward the net where he'll be in a fine position to finish off the point with a putaway volley. To make sure you get depth, hit your ground strokes high over the net—but not so high that they become floating mini-lobs. If you skim the ball over the net, your shots are likely either to drop short or end up in the net rather than over it.

Keep your opponent on the move by varying the placement of your ground strokes. Never let your opponent get in a groove. If you hit alternately to either corner, your opponent will soon see the pattern and begin to anticipate your next shot. So vary things. Hit some shots to alternate corners and hit others behind your opponent. Keep him guessing. If your opponent has a definite weakness, go for that, too.

When both of you are back on your baselines, your opponent may try moving you around the court in the hope of forcing an error. When that happens; hit straight back to the center of the baseline. That will reduce his possible angles of return and force him to hit back closer to you so you won't have to run far for the ball. And, of course, the deeper you hit your shots, the more difficulty your opponent will have in angling his returns.

2. Wait for a short ball

When you are faced with a steady baseliner, patience is the watchword. These players are able to get the ball back over the net with such regularity that you find yourself locked into interminable, mind-draining rallies.

Don't get itchy. Wait for a short ball—one that lands closer to the service line than the baseline on your side of the net. When it comes, move up quickly and hit an approach shot deep to keep your opponent behind the baseline. Then continue on up to the net so that you are in position to intercept your opponent's return with a volley. In fact, you should be able to end the point right there with a well-placed volley.

Even if you are playing on a slow clay court, you'll improve your chances of closing out the point by going in after a short ball.

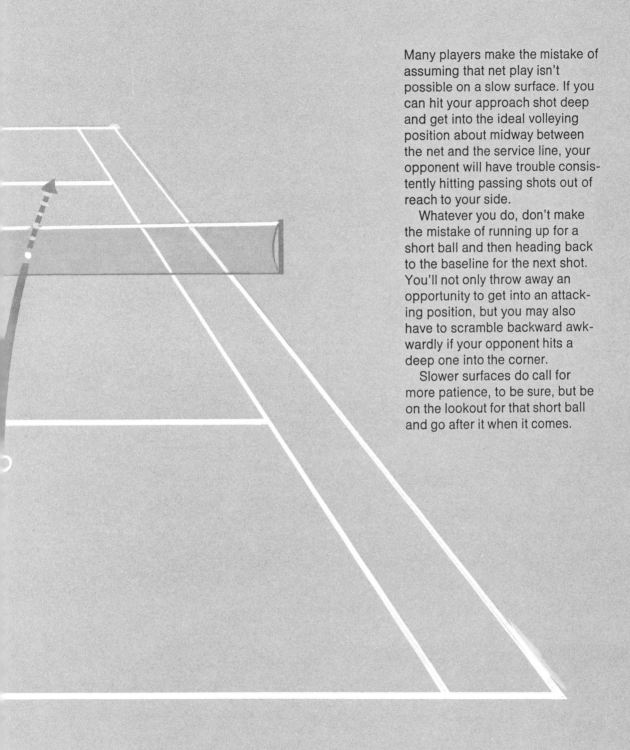

Many players make the mistake of assuming that net play isn't possible on a slow surface. If you can hit your approach shot deep and get into the ideal volleying position about midway between the net and the service line, your opponent will have trouble consistently hitting passing shots out of reach to your side.

Whatever you do, don't make the mistake of running up for a short ball and then heading back to the baseline for the next shot. You'll not only throw away an opportunity to get into an attacking position, but you may also have to scramble backward awkwardly if your opponent hits a deep one into the corner.

Slower surfaces do call for more patience, to be sure, but be on the lookout for that short ball and go after it when it comes.

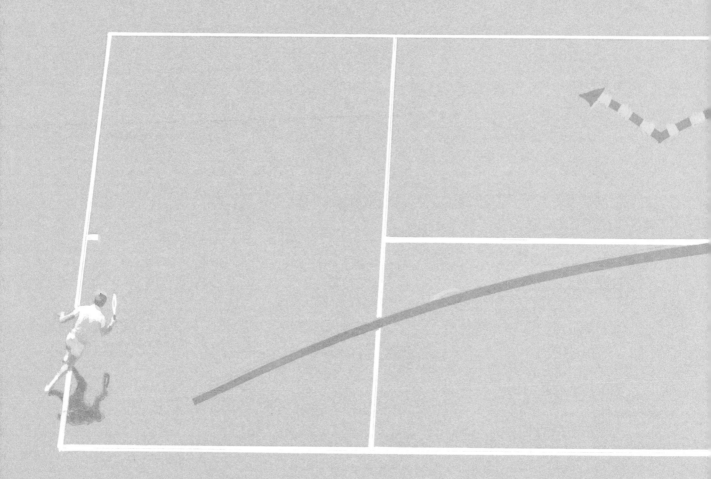

3. Change a losing game

What do you do about the human backboard? How do you handle the player who sits patiently on the baseline, returning ground stroke after ground stroke and lobs over your head every time you go to the net? That's the kind of player who waits for you to beat yourself, to make the errors that will give him the match.

The answer is to change your game and, as a result, force him to change his. For example, when you get a short ball, don't always hit an approach shot. Instead, hit a short ball yourself to force your opponent to come up to the net. The odds are that your opponent won't have a good volley. So you'll probably be able to win the point by forcing an error or by returning his weak volley as a passing shot to one side of him.

You are taking a risk, of course, that your opponent will come up, hit an approach and then take charge at the net. But the odds are against it. Most baseliners are not expert net-rushers or volleyers.

You might also consider changing your game by hitting a
drop shot, even though it's a fairly low percentage shot. Wait for
a really short ball, as shown here. With luck, your steady baseliner will be so surprised that he'll never get off the mark and
you'll win the point outright. Even if he does manage to
scramble up to retrieve it, the chances are that he'll either net
his return or hit a weak shot you can volley for a winner.

Don't tarry in no-man's land between the baseline and the
service line after you've hit the drop shot. Continue up to the
net and be ready to close out the point just as you would if you
had hit an approach shot. Remember, even if your opponent
does return your drop shot, he'll be in unfamiliar territory and
hitting up. So you'll have the upper hand when it comes to your
next shot.

Whichever tactic you choose to employ—a short ball or a
drop shot—you will succeed in changing the nature of your
game. You'll put the ground-stroker off his game and shift the
odds more in your favor.

4. Use a lob against a net-rusher

What about the player who keeps you on the baseline by rushing the net—not only after each serve but also after he returns your serve when you stay back? That type of player often wins points not so much on the strength of his play but simply because his constant net-rushing unnerves his opponent so much that he makes only tentative shots that can be easily volleyed away.

The solution is to keep the net-rushers away from the fore-court. Use your lob to force him back from the net. If he's a very aggressive player, he probably crowds the net where the volleys are easy to hit; that means he may have trouble getting

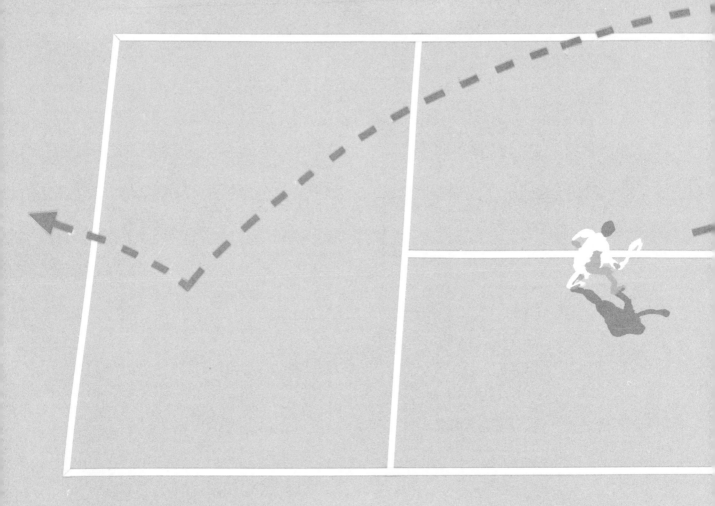

back in time to return your lob.

But what if your net-rushing opponent begins to back off from the net a bit to anticipate your lobs? So much the better. He won't be able to volley so effectively. And the farther he is from the net in the forecourt, the easier it will be for you to send passing shots past him down the line.

Don't forget, too, that a deep lob may elicit a weak return that will enable you to come up to the net. That gives you a chance to turn the tables on your opponent and force him to change his game. Even if you lack a strong net game, you'll have the advantage of surprise—and that will help you win the point.

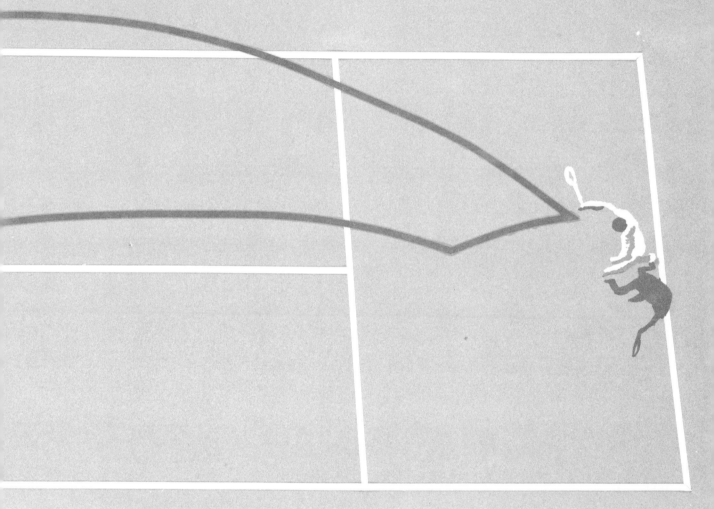

DOUBLES STRATEGY

HOW TO WIN AT DOUBLES

Doubles is the staple of tennis at the club level. It's a more social game than singles, less demanding physically and, because it allows more persons to play, is a special boon when court space is scarce. Yet despite its popularity, few players devote the time and thought to improving their doubles games that they do, for example, to working on their stroke-making.

To win consistently at doubles requires an understanding of court strategy that's fundamentally different from that used in singles. The differences start with the obvious facts that the court is larger in doubles and that there are twice as many players—and then go on from there to many less obvious, but critical, refinements.

This chapter details for you the strategy and some of the particular shots that are involved in successful doubles play. The first four

sections are illustrated with a series of court diagrams, accompanied by explanatory text, that take you through complete, typical points.

1. Get in position

The basic premise of doubles play—whether men's, women's or mixed—is that the team which controls the net usually wins the point. So begin each point with that goal in mind.

The server (A) should stand about halfway between the center mark and the singles sideline ready to follow his serve directly to the net. The server's partner (B) should take up the ideal net playing position about halfway between the service line and the net, standing a little closer to the singles sideline than to the center line. He should be able to cover the alley or the center of the court with only one step in either direction.

The receiver (C) should be positioned on the baseline close to the singles sideline when receiving in the deuce (or right-hand) court; he should be slightly more toward the center when receiving in the ad court. The receiver's first objective is to get the serve back and then think about going up to the net.

The receiver's partner (D) should stand with his heels just inside the service line closer to the center mark than to the singles sideline in order to protect against a volley made by the server's partner down the middle. As the receiver moves in after his return, the receiver's partner should move to the center of his half of the court and closer to the net.

2. Spin your serve

In doubles, you must get your first serve in. To do that, serve at about three-quarters of the speed you would use in singles and put plenty of spin on the ball to make sure that it curves into the service box. Use a slice serve such as Tony Trabert is demonstrating here. Swing your racquet across the back of the ball from left to right (if you're a right-hander). On contact, the racquet should go around the side of the ball to create the sidespin of the slice serve. A twist serve is also effective in doubles, especially on a second serve. But, unless you have a good one, stick to the slice and make sure you get the first one in.

3. Start with your stronger server

If your team has the choice, grab the advantage by serving first—unless you know your opponents warm up slowly, which could give you a chance to break serve in the first game. The more reliable server on your team should serve first, concentrating on getting his first serve in and keeping the ball in play. Don't be tempted to go for aces. Use a solid spin serve (see preceding page) and follow your serve to the net.

Serving with a purpose Following the action: the server spins his serve down the middle into the deuce court (A) and follows the ball toward the net (B and C) . . .

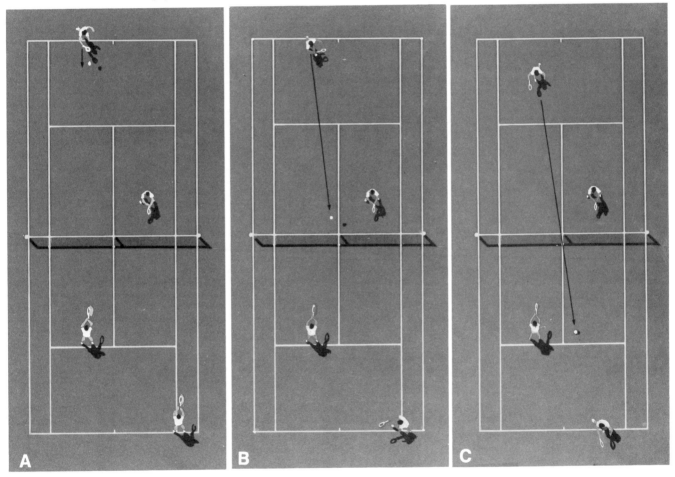

4. Go to the receiver's backhand

The majority of beginning and intermediate players will be weaker on the backhand, so you should aim for that side most of the time. Occasionally, though, go to the forehand to stop the receiver from anticipating a backhand and running around it. If you are facing a right-hander, serve down the center into the deuce, or right-hand, court (see C) and wide into the ad court. Serving down the center reduces the angle that the receiver can get on his return. A wide serve to the ad court will force the receiver to hit a backhand crosscourt shot. And that's tough to hit despite the greater choice of angle.

5. Put the bigger hitter in the ad court

Since doubles play calls for careful teamwork, spend time deciding your receiving positions. The player with the better forehand shouldn't always play in the deuce (or forehand) court and the better back-hander the ad court. The critical points will come when your opponents are serving into the ad court. So the player with the bigger, harder shots—the concluder— should play the ad court, while the more consistent player, the one who can be relied upon to keep the ball in play, should be in the deuce court. Also agree beforehand who will handle a shot coming down the middle. Generally, the player who is crosscourt from the opponent hitting the ball should take it since the ball will be coming toward him.

Receiving. . . Receiver replies with a backhand crosscourt (D) and begins to rush the net (E and F) . . .

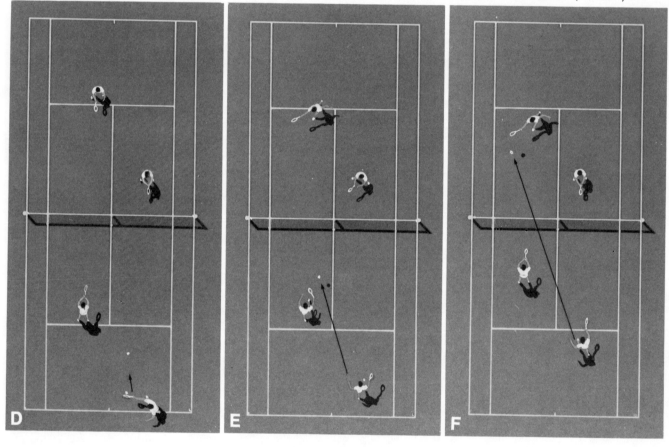

6. Don't move up too fast

Although the key to good doubles play is control of the net, especially for the serving team, don't rush headlong up to the net. You may put yourself out of position to make an effective shot on the way. The server should slow down momentarily in his run to the net somewhere around the service line (E), watch the receiver hit the ball and then move to meet it (F). Similarly, the receiver should slow down en route to the net so he can anticipate the opponents' reply to his service return.

7. Return crosscourt

When returning serve, go cross-court with a low ground stroke whenever you can—as Ron Holmberg is demonstrating here. Try to send the ball to the feet of the net-rushing server. He will then either have to volley up and present you with a set-up shot or, if the ball bounces, execute a difficult half volley. If you are pulled wide by the serve and can't return crosscourt effectively, a deep lob behind the net man is a good way to get back in the point. Resist the temptation to return serve down the line unless you're facing a net man who poaches effectively (that is, moves over frequently to cut off crosscourt returns with quick volleys). Going down the line is a low percentage shot because the ball crosses the highest part of the net, you have less margin for error and the net man will have an easy winner if he intercepts the ball.

8. Send the first volley deep

When serving and following the ball to the net, you're in the best position if the ball comes back high (G). That allows you to hit down directly at your opponent's feet. But if the receiver has returned low and crosscourt, you'll be forced to hit up. How can you make the best of the situation? If the receiver has stayed back, hit your volley deep to his side to keep him back on the baseline. If the receiver is coming in, hit the ball less hard so it will drop at his feet—and give him a tough shot. Don't aim the ball at the opposing net man since you'll hit up, giving him a set-up volley.

Putting the ball away . . . Server hits forehand volley (G) low at oncoming receiver who returns a weak backhand volley (H). Server closes in on net and hits a winning backhand volley (I) and (J).

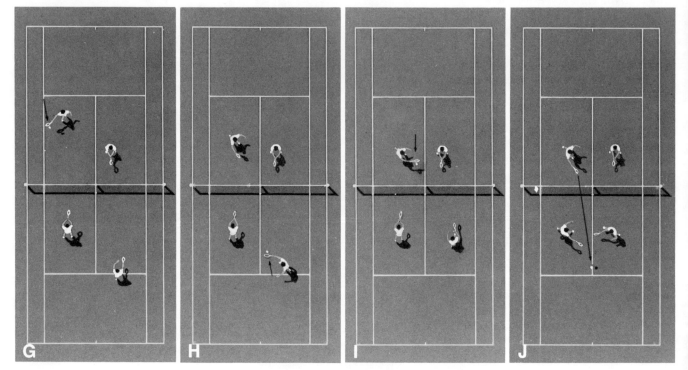

9. Hit down for a winner

Since doubles is a team game, you should work as a pair to set up situations where one partner can make the winning shot. For example, in the sequence above, the server's first volley (H) is low to the net-rushing receiver's feet, causing the receiver to volley up and hand a putaway opportunity to the server. Because the receiver has to hit up, the server can close in on the net (I) and hit a powerful volley down between his opponents (J) to win the point. So be content to keep the ball in play until you or your partner can set up a situation where one of you can hit a certain winner. When one of you strokes a ball which forces your opponent to hit up, be prepared to hit down for a winner on the next shot if you can.

10. Control your volleys

At the net, it often pays to go for control rather than power on volleys. If you hit the ball too hard, it will stay above the level of the net and give your opponents the opportunity to hit down. Your objective should be to keep the ball below your opponents' waist levels, thus forcing them to hit up to give you the easy shot. If both your opponents are close to the net, shorten your backswing to take some speed off the ball so it will drop toward their feet. Use a little backspin, if necessary, as Trabert is doing here. If both opponents are on the baseline, you can hit for more depth which will force them to stay back. Only when the ball comes to you well above the level of the net should you really hit the ball hard.

HOW TO SUCCEED AS A DOUBLES TEAM

Winning doubles calls for the two team members to work as one so that the combination results in better tennis than either could have produced alone. Good teamwork demands that you not only know your partner, but that you understand the principles of playing as a team.

1. Always play side by side

The essence of doubles play is that the partners should play as a unit. They should be side by side whenever possible. The team should also move from side to side together so that there are no more than 12 feet separating the partners. You can almost imagine the team connected by a loose rope which forces the players to move together up and back or from side to side.

2. Vary your serve

In doubles at the club level, a general rule is to serve to your opponent's backhand because most weekend players are weaker on that side. However, if you continually serve to your opponent's weaker side you can turn that weakness into a strength. If your opponent begins to expect a down-the-center serve in the deuce court, for instance, he will start edging over toward that side to get an early start on preparing for the return. So you should occasionally serve to your opponent's strength. A few serves to your opponent's forehand will stop him from cheating on his backhand and keep him guessing about your serving intentions.

Starting the point Following the action: the server aims wide to the receiver's forehand (A and B). The receiver replies with a defensive lob (C) . . .

A B C

3. Choose your service return carefully

The receiving partner has four options in returning serve: to hit crosscourt back to the oncoming server; to hit down the line past the net man; to hit a defensive lob deep to the opposing baseline, or to hit an offensive lob over the opposing net man. The best course is usually to hit crosscourt. But if you are facing a net man who persistently poaches to volley your service return, a down-the-line-shot will keep the poacher honest. The down-the-line return, though, has a lower percentage of success because it goes over the highest part of the net and you have less court to aim for. If you are drawn wide on return of serve, you should use the third option—a deep defensive lob. That will give you enough time to get back into the point and will also force the opposing team away from their commanding position at the net. The offensive lob is a low percentage shot, so it should be used only if you are certain that you can hit it properly.

4. Return a deep lob with a ground stroke

If your opponent tosses up a deep lob, you should always let it bounce before you make your shot. After all, there's always the chance that the lob will bounce out of court. More importantly, the ball will be moving more slowly after the bounce and, as a result, will present an easier target. However, the chances are that you'll be behind the baseline at this point, so it's not always advisable to try to smash the ball. That's a low percentage shot for the average player at such a distance from the net. Instead, let the ball fall from the highest point of its bounce and hit your strongest possible ground stroke, as Seixas is demonstrating here. You'll have plenty of time to get set for the hit and you may be able to pass your opponents with a powerful shot if you can keep it down the middle and fairly low over the net. Don't take any risks with this shot—your objective is to stay in the point long enough to get your team back up to the net.

5. Cover the court together

If your partner has to go back to the baseline to cover a very deep lob, you should not remain up at the net. If you do, there will be a large hole between you and your partner where one of your opponents can put away a well-placed shot. So when your partner goes back, retreat with him to give your team the best court coverage. Although retreating to the baseline will put you in a defensive position, you should be able to return to the net as soon as either of you gets a short ball. When that happens, both of you should move up together.

Working as a team ... The serving team retreats, allows the ball to bounce and returns a forehand drive (D) which is volleyed by receiver (E). His shot lands deep in the opposite court (F) ...

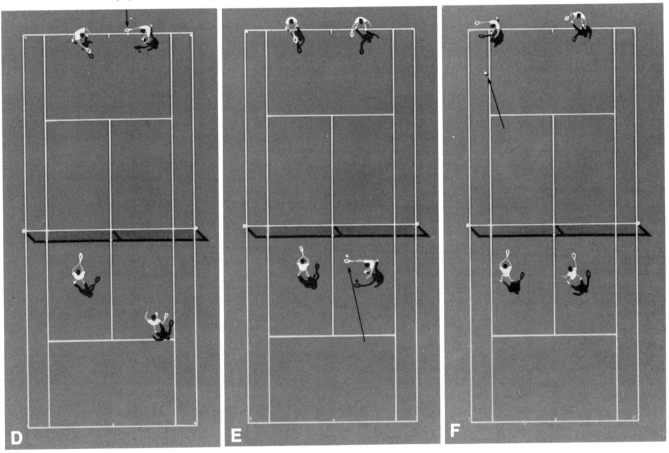

6. Move across the court in tandem

When you and your partner are both up at the net, try to anticipate the direction of your opponents' shots and move to cover them. If a player in the deuce court volleys a ball cross-court to the left (see diagram F), his team can expect that an attempted passing shot will probably be returned to the left side. So his partner should shift toward the left sideline to cover such a return. Doing that, of course, will open a gap in the middle of the court, so the player on the right should then move to the left, too. There should be a continuous lateral movement of both team members as the volleys go back and forth across the net. When at the net, after your shot—move either to recover your position or in the direction of the anticipated return.

7. Smash for a winner off a short lob

Whenever your opponents hit a low lob which falls between the net and the middle of the "no-man's land" between the service line and the baseline, you should go for a winning overhead smash. Be prepared to take the ball on the fly so that your opponents will have little time to get ready for your smash. If you have the control, hit the ball away from your opponents to prevent them from scrambling and returning a defensive lob which would keep them in the point. Hitting a good overhead calls for rapid footwork so you can get behind the oncoming lob. Make small adjustments in your position as the ball is falling and meet it with the center of your racquet, as Holmberg is doing here, with a slight wrist snap which will bring the ball down sharply into your opponents' court. Keep your eyes on the ball throughout the stroke, resisting the temptation to drop your head as you hit the ball.

8. When to lob offensively

An offensive lob is an excellent weapon for getting your opponents away from the net—provided that you catch them by surprise and execute the shot properly. When you use an offensive lob, you should be well inside the baseline where you might hit a passing shot if the other team was not crowding the net. The lob should look like a passing shot until the last moment when you lift the ball up so that it just passes over your opponent's reach. It should then drop so that the other team has little time to scramble back and make any kind of return. Never attempt to use an offensive lob unless you also have the choice of a passing shot.

Using the lob ... The server attempts a forehand lob (G) which drops short (H) and is smashed by receiver (I) to win the point.

9. Take care of your own lobs

As a general rule, each player should attempt to smash back the lobs that come to his side of the court. The only exceptions to this rule are: when one player has an exceptionally poor overhead; when one player is very close to the net and his partner is still back (which would be the case, for example, with a lobbed return of service); or when wind moves the ball sideways across the court. If one player does cross over to the other half of the court to hit an overhead, he should holler, "Mine," so that he and his partner don't get tangled up going for the ball. And his partner should immediately scurry to cover the side of the court that's been left vacated. However, it's best to develop the habit of running back for lobs on your side.

HOW TO POACH

1. Decide before you serve

Poaching—the movement of the net man laterally across the court to volley away the receiver's crosscourt return of serve—demands quick thinking and fast footwork on the part of the serving team. So it's important that both of them agree beforehand that the net man will try a poach if the receiver hits a crosscourt return of serve. Some doubles teams like to use signals; the net man puts his hand behind his back and indicates to the server by a closed or open fist whether or not he will poach. It's better, though, for the partners to make the decision verbally before they take their positions. And once they make it, they must stick to the decision.

Going for a poach Following the action: the server hits into the deuce court (A). The receiver returns low and crosscourt (B and C) . . .

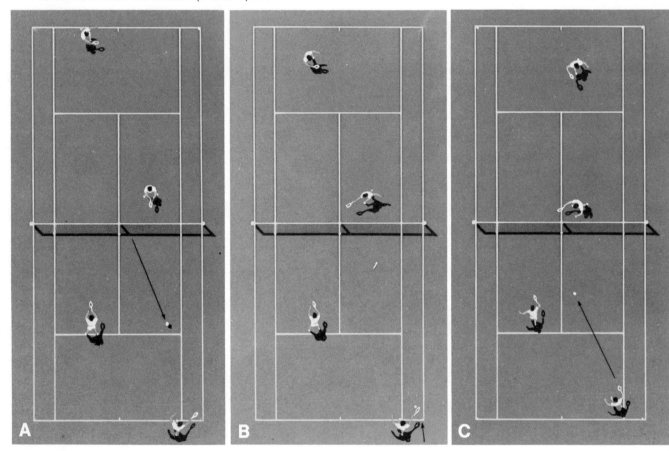

A B C

2. Cover the empty court

As the net man moves over to cut off the return of serve, he will leave his half of the court unguarded. So the server should not run directly up to the net after his serve. Instead, he should take a few steps forward, cross over into the court his partner has vacated and begin moving toward the net on that half of the court. The poacher, of course, should continue into the server's court after volleying the return of serve. The scissors action of the two players will insure that the court is covered in case the receiver sends his return down the line or in case the poacher does not put the ball away with his first volley.

3. Get an early start

When poaching, you must make your move the moment the receiver hits the ball. Wait with your weight forward, prepared to push off and to reach the ball for a volley. Don't telegraph your intention by moving before the receiver hits the ball. If the receiver realizes that you are going to poach, he'll try for a down-the-line return and perhaps hit a winner. So wait until the receiver makes contact. Then, if you are moving to the right, push off on your left foot and take a few quick steps to get into position to cut off the return. Most players prefer to poach on their forehand sides because it is easier to stretch out for a forehand than a backhand volley. But whether you go for a forehand or a backhand poach, always get a fast start.

4. Stay back against a poacher

Both the receiver and the receiver's partner should hold their positions when the opposing net man poaches. If you're the receiver's partner and you move toward the net, the poacher can hit the ball down at your feet where you will have difficulty making much of a return. If you're the receiver and you run up toward the net, the poacher can hit the ball either at your feet or between you and your partner. Either way, you're in trouble. If you stay back, you'll have more time to reach the ball and, perhaps, get a chance to toss up a lob to stay in the point.

Putting the ball away . . . The net man drifts sideways to poach as the server crosses behind him to cover the unguarded court (D). The poaching net man hits a volley (E) for a winner (F).

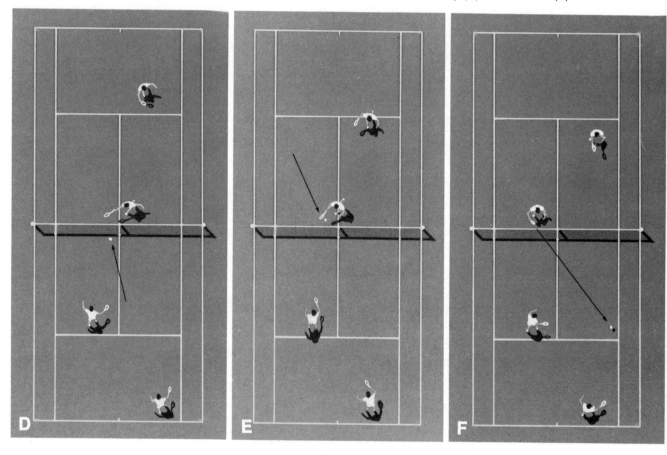

5. Defend with a down-the-line shot

If you consistently return serve crosscourt, the opposing team will start to anticipate that and poach on your returns. So once the opposition begins to poach, you should go for a down-the-line return to keep the net man honest. You might also try an offensive lob over the head of the net man. If the net man knows that you can lob effectively, that will keep him back from the net and so reduce the chances of his making a successful poach. Don't change your mind, however, about your return just because you see a slight movement on the part of the poacher—he may be faking a poach in the hope of causing you to muff your return as you try to change a crosscourt shot into a down-the-line shot.

6. Hit down for a winning poach

For a successful poach, you must hit the ball while it is higher than the net. That means moving up close to the ball and the net so that you can hit down. The closer you are to the net, the higher the ball and the easier the volley. However, don't get so close that you hit the net with your racquet when you make the shot—under the rules, you lose that point even if the shot itself is good. Aim your volley at the opposing net man's feet or hit the ball into the open court where your opponents will have a problem making any sort of return. Hit your volley hard to finish the point right there.

HOW TO SET UP A WINNER

1. Use your team's strengths

In well-balanced doubles teams at any level, one player is usually better at "touch," or placing the ball, while the other player hits with more power. When that's the case, the team should work to set up points by using the touch player to force the other team into making a defensive shot. The stronger player can then act as a "concluder" and put the weak shot away with a stinging volley. When your team is receiving, it's best for the touch player to play the deuce, or right-side, court while the stronger player takes the ad court. In that way, he will often be responsible for winning the more critical points—ad out, 30-40, etc.

Hitting short Following the action from mid-point with all four players at the net: Player 1 hits a soft shot (A) which drops short (B), forcing player 2 to move forward and hit up (C) . . .

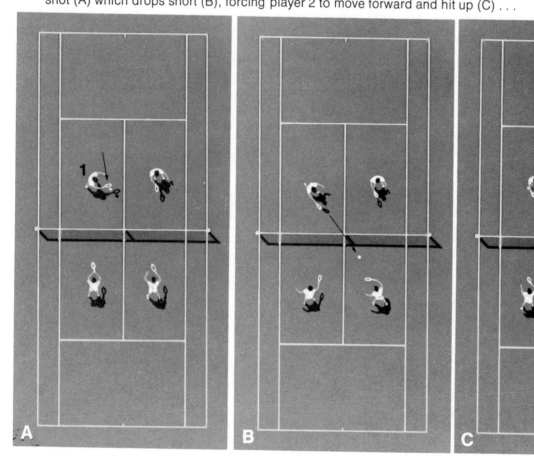

2. Watch the ball

When all four players are at the net, the shots come so rapidly that reactions have to be almost instinctive. But no matter how quick your reflexes are, you won't be able to hit the ball unless you keep your eyes on it all the time. At the net, watch the ball and not the other players. In fact, you should be concentrating so hard that you'd be able to read the label on the ball if it wasn't spinning through the air. You'll find that your eye contact will improve if you try to hit the ball out in front of you. If you allow the ball to get to your side, the chances of a mis-hit will increase. Crouching down to get your eyes closer to the level of the ball's flight will help you follow the ball better and make a better shot.

3. Hit at your opponent's feet
To set up a winning shot when all four players are at the net,
hit a short ball aimed at an opponent's feet. Instead of volleying
hard, take some pace off the ball and hit down, preferably with
a little underspin so that the ball drops sharply after crossing
the net. If the ball is going down as it crosses the net, your
opponent will be forced to lift the ball up just to get it back.
You or your partner can then move in for a putaway volley.

4. Get down for a low volley

When an opponent hits a low shot that dips below the top of the net, you will be forced to hit up to get the ball back. Although you're in a defensive position, you can make the best of it by hitting the ball just hard enough so it barely clears the net before dropping toward your opponent's feet. To hit such a shot, you must get down low with your eyes close to the flight of the ball. Bend your knees and keep your racquet head up. Hit the ball firmly, but without a long backswing and with no follow-through. If you hit the ball too hard, it will rise up over the net and your opponents will have an easy setup. Concentrate on keeping the ball low over the net.

5. Aim at the closest opponent

After you have set things up so that your opponents have to hit up at the net, you should be in a position to win the point with a volley. If your opponents are well up close to the net, hit your volley down at the feet of the player nearest you. Most players can't return a hard shot hit directly at their feet. On the other hand, at those times you have to hit the ball when it is lower than the net, you should always aim the ball at the opponent who's farther away from you. The ball will have farther to go and will be lower before the other player has a chance to hit it.

Finishing off the point . . . As the ball crosses the net (D), player 3 moves up to hit down the middle (E) for a putaway volley (F).

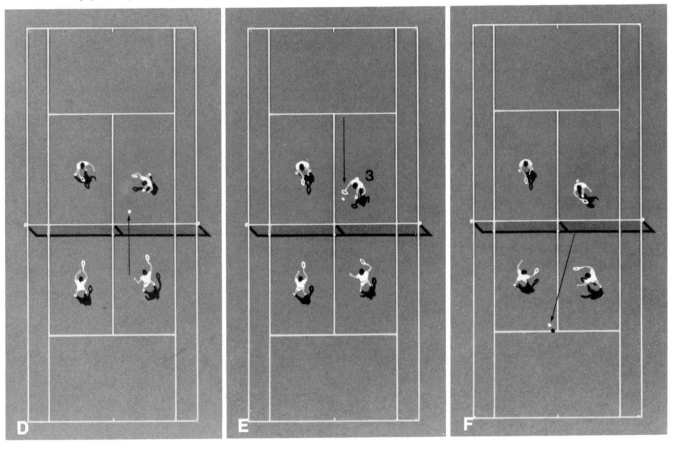

1. Get your first serve in with spin and depth.
2. Return serve low and cross-court to the server's feet.
3. Move in line with your partner to cover the court—forward, back and laterally.
4. Always try to control the net position.
5. Force your opponents to hit up.

HOW TO BLUNT A STRONG SERVE

Retreat to return serve

When you are facing a server with a hard delivery that lands so consistently deep you barely have time to get your racquet on the ball, step back three or four feet behind the baseline. The extra distance will give you a little more time to position yourself and to make your stroke. You might also take a shorter backswing because you'll have little time to make your return and you don't need the power of a long, flowing ground stroke. You can use the speed that the server puts on the ball. You should step back before the server prepares to hit the ball. Be prepared to move forward, however, because a crafty server might decide to drop a serve close to the net, forcing you to run up for the return. Stand back against a hard server and you'll find that a difficult serve will be a lot easier to handle.

Lob over the net player

If one or both members of the other team are serving well and coming to the net successfully, return occasionally by sending a lob over the head of the server's partner. Use an offensive lob that just clears the net player's outstretched arm and racquet. You'll usually catch the other team going the wrong way. Instead of rushing the net, they'll have to scramble back to cover the lob. At best, you'll win the point outright. At the very least, you'll put your opponents on the defensive instead of allowing them to continue the attack. The server will think twice about continuing a serve-and-volley game and the net player will be kept guessing.

HOW TO THWART A GOOD SERVICE RETURN

Stay back and hit a ground stroke

When you're serving, you may run into trouble if the receiver consistently returns crosscourt to your feet as you follow your serves to the net. If you can't get close enough to the net to volley and are forced to hit difficult half volleys, the thing to do is to stay back at the baseline and hit the ball crosscourt to the receiver's feet. That will stop the receiver from rushing the net behind his return. If the receiver tries to come in behind the return, a low, crosscourt shot will force him to hit up and give you a chance to put away a winner. So when you are facing a receiver with a good return of serve, stay back and use your strongest ground stroke.

Use the Australian formation

If the returns of serve come crosscourt so low that the incoming server has a hard time getting a racquet on the ball, try placing the net player on the same half of the court as the server. This alignment is often called the Australian formation. The net player will then be in a position to volley the crosscourt return right back at the opposing net man and, most likely, will win the point. The result usually will be that the receiver will be pressured into returning down the line—a more difficult shot with a higher percentage of error. When a doubles team uses the Australian formation, the server should stand close to the center mark so that he can run into the opposite, uncovered half of the court to handle a down-the-line return. The object of the Australian formation is both to counter an effective cross-court return and to get the receiver out of a stroking groove. When that has been done, the serving team can revert to the conventional formation. To defend against the Australian formation, you must either have a reliable down-the-line service return or resort to a quick lob over the head of the net player into the part of the court just vacated by the server. Don't let the unusual formation confuse you; decide on a course of action and stick to it.

LEFT-HANDERS

THE LEFT-HANDED GAME: HOW TO PLAY IT, HOW TO COUNTER IT

Through the ages, left-handers have often been cruelly slighted in a world where everything—from scissors and wrist watches to gear shifts and school desks—seems to be designed for right-handers. But the left-handers reap their revenge on the tennis court by the changes they force on the games of righties of comparable abilities.

The right-hander finds that his opponent's slice serve now curves the other way, the forehand is on the other side, and so on. So he has to adjust his game while the left-hander simply plays normally—unless he meets another left-handed opponent, of course.

On the following pages, we'll show those of you who are left-handed how to capitalize on your advantage. We'll also show you, on opposing pages, how a right-hander can counter the particular strengths of the typical left-handed player.

FOR THE LEFT-HANDER

THE SERVE
Spin your deliveries

Left-handers should cultivate a good slice serve, especially for the second serve, since the ball will break in just the opposite direction from what the right-hander has become used to in facing other right-handers. It will, thus, often catch him badly prepared. Naturally, as a lefty, you should aim the majority of your serves at the right-hander's weakness—usually the backhand.

For example, when serving into the ad or left-hand court (see the diagram on the right), aim close to the singles sideline so that you pull your opponent wide out of court on his backhand. However, when serving into the deuce court, you should also aim most of your serves close to the sideline so that they break into the body of the receiver and cramp his forehand stroke.

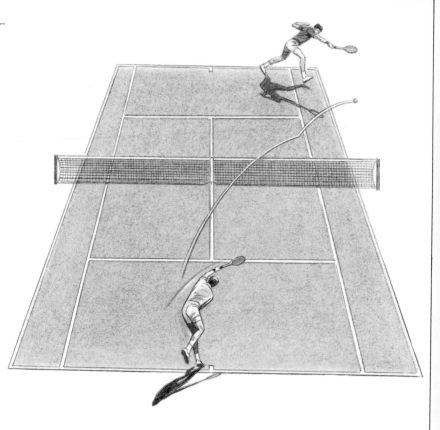

RETURN OF SERVE
Mix things up

When you are facing a right-handed server, you may get many serves on your forehand side; that's because the server is used to aiming at right-handed opponents' backhands—which is, of course, your forehand side. So take advantage of those serves to your forehand by mixing up your returns to give your opponent maximum trouble.

The safest return, when your opponent stays back, is cross-court and deep. But when you are in the ad court, go down the line occasionally (see A on the right) or crosscourt and shallow (B). By using all the angles on your service returns, you'll keep the server guessing and, perhaps, make him reluctant to follow his serve to the net.

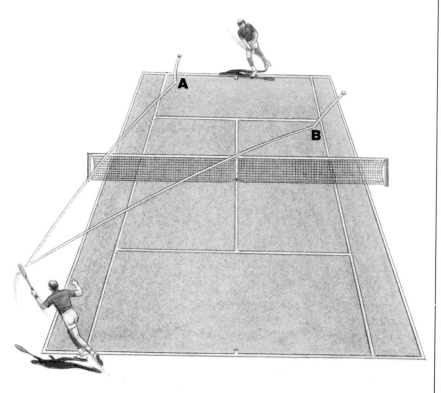

AGAINST THE LEFT-HANDER

THE SERVE
Change your placement

When serving against a lefty, remember to reverse the majority of your placements. For instance, instead of serving down the center into the deuce court (see A at the right) as you might do to a right-hander with a weak backhand, slice your serve wide into the deuce court (B) to the lefty's backhand. Similarly, most of your serves into the ad court should go down the center if your left-handed opponent has a relatively weak backhand.

Many left-handers seem to have strong forehands—perhaps because right-handers unwittingly hit to that side out of habit. So it will pay you to avoid the forehand side on most of your serves. Adjust your serve to attack the weaker side, as you would against a right-hander.

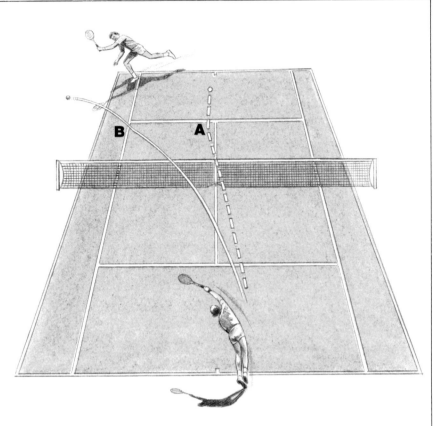

RETURN OF SERVE
Stay away from the ball

Returning serve against a left-hander is a little like playing in the wind—the ball comes at you differently. When a lefty slices a serve into the deuce court close to the singles sideline (see right), the ball will curve into your body instead of breaking away as a right-hander's slice serve does. A ball that breaks toward your body usually will force a cramped and, most likely, off-balance stroke.

So you should stay away from the ball by changing the place where you wait to receive serve. In the deuce court, stand a foot or two closer to the center mark than for a right-hander. In the ad court, stand closer to, or even straddling, the singles sideline so you can return serve with the ball well away from your body.

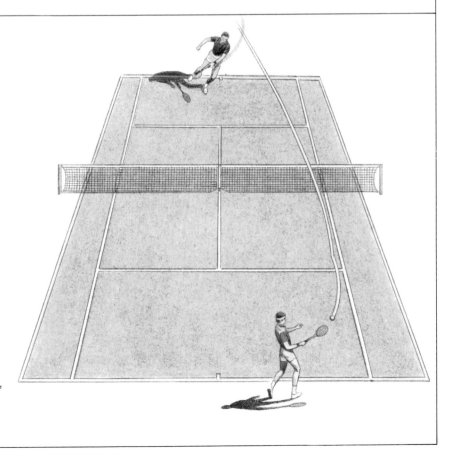

GROUND STROKES
Use your forehand

Many lefties have much better forehands than backhands. If your forehand is a powerful weapon, use it as much as possible. Try favoring your forehand when waiting to receive serve by edging over so that most of the serves come on your forehand side. On weaker second serves, you can run around your backhand and take the serve on your more powerful forehand.

Your game will improve, especially on passing shots, if you can use topspin on your forehand. The topspin will help bring the ball down in your opponent's court so that you can hit your forehands as hard as you wish without as much risk of the ball going out of court. However, don't become overly dependent on your forehand; work on your backhand, too.

Guillermo Vilas

APPROACH SHOTS
Send the ball deep

As a rule, it's best to hit most of your forehand approach shots down the line so that you'll have less of an angle to cover as you continue up to the net. A cross-court shot would leave you open to a down-the-line passing shot. But as a lefty, your forehand approach down the line will go to a right-hander's forehand where he may be able to reply with a hard passing shot.

So keep your approach shots deep to give yourself a little extra time to get into the proper volleying position. A backhand approach shot down the line will, of course, also go to a right-hander's backhand where there's less possibility of a strong passing shot. However, you should keep your approach shots deep on both sides.

Jimmy Connors

AGAINST THE LEFT-HANDER

GROUND STROKES
Go for the weakness

When you are playing a left-hander from the baseline, use high percentage shots. Keep your ground strokes deep and send most of them crosscourt. On your forehand (see right), a deep crosscourt shot will go to a lefty's backhand, generally the weaker side. If you can move the lefty wide on his backhand, you may force an error or a weak return that you can easily put away.

It's equally important that your backhands be deep enough to keep a left-handed opponent behind the baseline, since a crosscourt backhand will go to the lefty's forehand where he could hit a strong forehand approach on a shorter ball. Try for consistency on your ground strokes so that the lefty makes most of the errors.

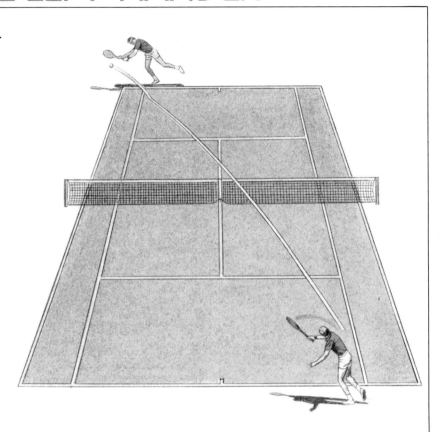

APPROACH SHOTS
Hit to the backhand

Most right-handers prefer to hit their approach shots down the line, especially on the forehand side. However, a forehand approach down the line to a lefty (see A on the right) would go to his forehand, usually his strongest side. So if you are playing a left-hander with a relatively weak backhand, hit your approach shots mostly to that weakness.

Go crosscourt with your forehand approach (B) but move over a little to the left of the center line to cover a possible attempt by the lefty at a backhand down-the-line passing shot. On the backhand side, of course, your approach shots can be made down the line to the lefty's backhand.

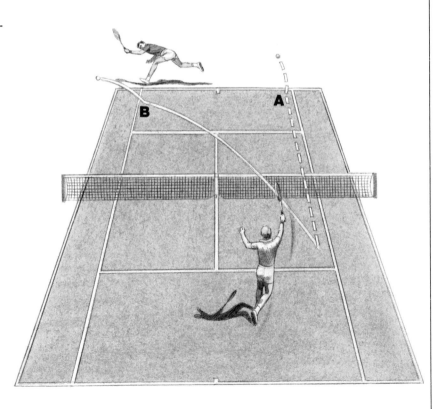

PRACTICE & CONDITIONING

HOW TO IMPROVE YOUR TENNIS PLAY

Unlike the professionals, most average tennis players cannot play the sport for several hours every day. So if you wish to play your best tennis, you should practice, both on and off the court and you should keep in shape with a regular conditioning program. This chapter will show you ways to practice on the court with a partner, ways to practice at home or when a court is not available and some special tennis exercises that should form part of your usual conditioning program. By practicing and staying in shape, you'll be better able to play your best tennis every time you go out on court.

SIX WAYS TO BUILD A BETTER GAME

The fastest, surest way to improve at tennis is, of course, to practice—whether you're a tyro or a touring pro. But the practice must have a purpose. It's pointless to go out on court and simply hit balls from baseline to baseline as though you were having an extended warm-up session. For a practice to be meaningful, you should work on specific parts of your game and, preferably, have some way of measuring your improvement.

What, then, is the best way to practice? On the following pages, the Advisory Board offers six on-court practice routines that they feel will be most helpful to players at almost any level of the game. Each member describes his own favorite routine developed, in most cases, after many years of teaching tennis.

Use these routines by setting up regular practice sessions—perhaps with your usual doubles partner. Pick out the routines that will best strengthen the weaker parts of your game and then make them tougher as your game improves. The more time you can give to purposeful practice the better, but an hour or so at least three times a week should be enough to help you build a better game.

Vic Seixas:
Drill with complimentary strokes

If you want to concentrate on one particular shot in your practice session, set up a routine which allows your partner to work on a complementary shot at the same time. For instance, if you'd like to practice your serve (above), that gives your partner a good opportunity to practice his return of serve (below). Tell him in advance whether you are going to aim for his forehand or his backhand to permit him to focus strictly on stroking. Then, switch around so that you both get a turn at serving and receiving.

Similarly, you can practice lobs and overheads or ground strokes and volleys as complementary shots. But make sure you have plenty of balls on hand so that you can keep the action going steadily.

Tony Trabert: Develop consistency by counting shots

Many weekend players have trouble simply keeping the ball in play. This routine will help you build consistency in a competitive way.

See how many times you can hit the ball back and forth over the net without making an error. Keep a count and try to break your own records. At first, you may be able to keep the ball going for only three or four returns. But before you know it, you'll soon be surpassing 50 and then maybe 100.

Start out with, say, crosscourt forehands (above) and then move on to a crosscourt backhand series (below). Later, you can try to move your practice partner around the court. Concentrate on early preparation, a solid hit and a good follow-through. Don't try to beat your partner; instead aim for steady, consistent shots that you'll be able to rely on in a match.

Ron Holmberg: Work on your weakest shots

Most of your practice sessions should be devoted to the shots that you don't like to hit because they are usually the weakest parts of your game. For example, many weekend players have such poor overheads that they let lobs bounce in order to take them as ground strokes. Have your partner lift some easy lobs close to the net so you can hit them on the fly (above).

If your net game is weak, have your partner take a bucket of balls and send you a series of balls slow enough for you to volley (below). Practice your weakness —but spend some time working on your strengths, of course, or they may also become weaknesses.

Roy Emerson:
Improve your accuracy
with half-court drills

There are many half-court drills
that will help your game but I
prefer to have one player in the
volleying position inside the
service box and the other player
on the baseline in the opposite
corner (above). The volleyer
should try to hit all his shots deep
into the corner while the baseliner
tries to pass the volleyer.

You can either play a game of
keeping the ball going as long as
possible or you can play a sort of
mini-tennis using only half the
court (the shaded areas of the
courts here are ''out''). Change
positions from time to time to play
both backhand and forehand
corners (below) and to let both
players work at the net.

George Lott:
Play two-on-one
for better doubles

The best way to practice doubles is by playing the game, but if you have only three players you can get in some useful practice by going two-on-one. Two players hit ground strokes from the baseline while the net player replies with series of volleys (above). The net player should concentrate on keeping his volleys deep so that the action can be continuous.

When the net player's volleys become grooved, the baseliners can try to pass him by hitting faster-paced balls or an occasional lob. The two-on-one routine is particularly grueling for the net player, so rotate the positions frequently(below) or the net player will soon become exhausted.

Bill Price:
Use table tennis scoring
for ground-stroking

With players who want to work on their ground strokes, I often suggest that they play a game, scored like table tennis to 21 points, in which each ball must land between the service line and the baseline to be good. That helps groove the depth you want on ground strokes. You can play this game with shots that are all cross-court (above) or all down the line (below), depending on the strokes that you wish to practice.

With beginners, I recommend that they forgo the conventional serve and merely start the point by dropping the ball and hitting it. With the better players, it's possible to make the routine tougher by requiring each player to hit the ball behind a line drawn midway between the service line and the baseline (below).

FIVE OFF-COURT ROUTINES TO UPGRADE YOUR GAME

Your best route to better tennis is to practice regularly on court with a partner. But if you can't get a court or are on your own, you can still polish parts of your game with the simple, off-court routines shown on these pages.

If you spend a few minutes a day off court doing one or more of these routines, you will soon find that you're playing better when you get back on court.

1. Use a mirror to check your swing

Stand in front of a large mirror so that you can get a full-length view of yourself as you run through your strokes, as Vic Seixas is doing here. Check the position of your racquet at the farthest point of your backswing, at the point of contact with the ball and at the completion of your follow-through. Repeat each stroke until you have an image in your mind of the correct way to hit the ball. Then, when you are out on court and your strokes go awry, try to recall that image. It should help you regroove your swing.

You can use the mirror to show you positions that should eventually become instinctive. For example, many players take the racquet back too high on the forehand. Check in the mirror to see where your racquet is when you take it back quickly. If it's too high, adjust your swing and keep working on it in front of the mirror until you've got the proper motion grooved.

2. Make your ball release more consistent

Unless you have a consistent ball release, you will never develop a reliable serve. You can get that consistency by practicing the ball release at home in a room with a high ceiling or outdoors close to a building or the fence around a tennis court, as George Lott is demonstrating. Check the height of your ball contact point by stretching up and slightly forward with your racquet. Note where the point is in relation to your ceiling or some part of the outdoor wall or court fence and practice your release so that the ball always rises to the contact point.

When you can lift the ball to the same point each time, swing your racquet without hitting the ball as an aid to improving your service rhythm. In fact, you might let the ball fall to the ground as a check to make sure that you are releasing the ball in front and a little to the side of your body.

3. Groove your strokes at the backboard

You can put in more concentrated practice against a proper tennis backboard or even just a flat wall than you can in the same time on a tennis court. Almost any stroke can be practiced against the backboard. But the secret to getting the most out of a backboard drill is not to hit the ball too hard. Many players like to wallop the ball—with the result that it comes back so fast they don't have time to prepare correctly for the next stroke.

Stand about 30 feet from the wall when practicing ground strokes. Take a full backswing and follow through completely. Your goal should be to reproduce a consistent stroke. Aim for a fixed target on the wall and count the number of direct hits that you score.

You can also practice against the backboard with a partner, as Ron Holmberg and Tony Trabert are showing here. Hitting with a partner approximates the rhythm of a tennis game and usually forces you to move after the ball, as you do in a match, instead of hitting from the same position all the time.

4. Bounce the ball for better control

Anytime that you have a racquet in your hand, you can improve your hand and eye coordination by simply bouncing the ball in the air or on the ground with your racquet, as Bill Price is doing. Play a game with yourself to see how many times you can bounce the ball without missing. You may find it more difficult at first than you had imagined because, although the exercise looks simple, consistency isn't always easy to attain. The bouncing drill can also improve your feel for the ball on the racquet.

If you want to develop the degree of touch that you need for a drop shot, try throwing the ball in the air and catching it on your racquet with almost no bounce. That's harder than it looks, too.

5. Speed up your game with shadow stroking

Shadow stroking is practicing imaginary tennis strokes and footwork off-court with a racquet but without a ball, as Roy Emerson is demonstrating. You can do it in your basement, on the driveway or when you are waiting for a court. Imagine that you are playing out a complete point and call out the strokes to yourself as you move.

For example, you might serve, follow your serve toward the net, pause for the first volley, move up for the next volley, retreat for a smash and then move up again for a putaway volley. Move as quickly as possible with short steps and sideways skips. Be sure to execute all your strokes fully and with imaginary ball contact out in front of you. As a variation, you can have a friend call out the strokes that you should hit. That should really keep you on your toes.

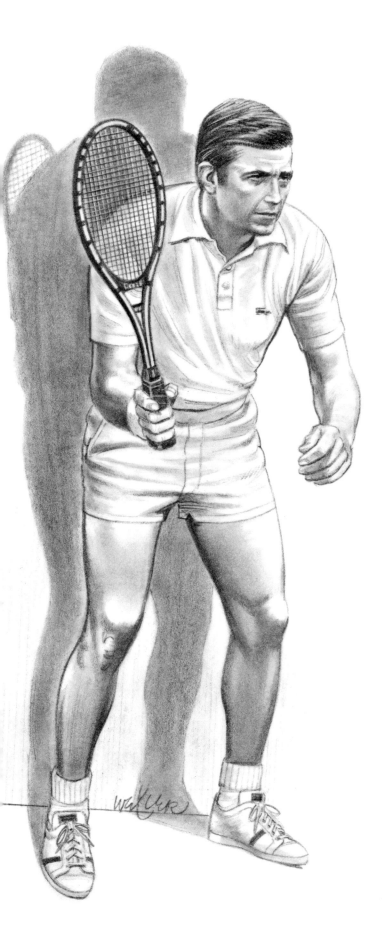

6. Practice volleys with your back

Many weekend tennis players have trouble hitting crisp volleys because they take too long a swing at the ball. If you have a long backswing on your volleys, the ball will be upon you faster than you can swing the racquet forward and the usual result is a mis-hit or even a complete miss. The cure is to practice stroking your volleys with your back to the wall. The wall will stop you from taking the racquet back farther than your shoulder. You can then punch forward at an imaginary ball with a short stroke. This is an exercise you can do whenever you have a few minutes to spare —at home or even up against the wire fence as you wait for your turn on court.

HOW TO SHAPE UP TO PLAY YOUR BEST TENNIS

To do your best on court, you should get in shape to play tennis and not play tennis to get in shape. It's a sport that demands stamina, agility and muscle strength. Those qualities can best be achieved through a regular conditioning program which includes exercises like the ones shown in this section.

Every player's exercise needs are different, of course, so you should work out a program that suits your capabilities. If you have doubts about your ability to perform any of the exercises suggested, consult your physician before attempting them.

1. Run for speed and stamina

If you can do no other exercise, regular running will help your tennis game the most. It will build up your heart and lungs, and strengthen your leg muscles at the same time.

However, simple jogging alone is not sufficient for tennis. You can improve your agility and increase your stamina by doing a series of short wind sprints. Run the length of a tennis court as fast as you can, as Roy Emerson is doing here; pause or run slowly until you catch your breath, and then do it again. Start with five wind sprints, building up until you can do 20 or more.

If running doesn't appeal to you, try bicycling.

2. Skip rope for faster footwork

Swift footwork is one of the cornerstones of a good tennis game. You must be able to start and stop quickly to get into the proper position to hit the ball. You should be constantly on the balls of your feet.

Jumping rope, as Ron Holmberg is demonstrating here, will both speed up your footwork and build your stamina. If you can, perform the exercise by swinging the rope both forward and backward. Start with two minutes per day and build up to five minutes—with a few pauses to catch your breath, if need be.

If you dislike skipping rope, you can improve your footwork by running around a row of tennis balls placed about six feet apart on a court or on your driveway. Run in and out of the line like a skier on a slalom course.

3. Use isometrics to build muscles

You can strengthen your shoulder, arm and wrist muscles any time you have a spare moment by doing suitable isometric exercises. In these exercises, the muscles simply push against each other or a fixed object with almost no movement of the arm or body.

For example, as Vic Seixas is showing here, you can make a fist with one hand and push against the flat palm of the other hand. Do it for a count of 10 and then reverse hands.

You can perform this exercise while watching television or sitting at your desk. Or you can modify the exercise by pushing on the steering wheel of your car while waiting for a light.

4. Stretch your leg muscles for flexibility

Many weekend tennis players have poor mobility, and a few even suffer sprains because their leg muscles aren't flexible enough. You can acquire that flexibility by stretching your leg muscles the way Tony Trabert is doing here.

Lean forward on one knee with the other leg straight out behind you. Stretch gently without bouncing and hold the position for a count of five. Then reverse legs and repeat the exercise. Go gently at first with three or four repetitions and build up to 10.

This exercise is also a fine way to limber up before you go out on court for a match. It warms up your leg muscles and, thus, reduces the possibility that you'll pull a muscle by pushing yourself too hard in the first few games.

5. Strengthen your stomach muscles for powerful serves

Your stomach and back muscles take a lot of punishment when you serve, so your conditioning program should include one or more exercises for those muscles. One of the most effective is the V-up, demonstrated here by Vic Seixas.

Start from a sitting position with your legs stretched out in front of you and your arms by your side. Raise your legs, keeping them as straight as possible and attempt to touch your toes with your fingertips. Don't worry if you can't do it at first. You can make the exercise harder by starting from a prone position.

Sit-ups and push-ups will also strengthen your back and stomach muscles. Be careful, though; these kinds of exercises are strenuous. So if you have any history of back problems, consult a physician first.

ART/PHOTO CREDITS

All illustrations by Elmer Wexler, except the following by Dick Kohfield: 156-7, 158-9, 160-173, 175, 178, 181, 183, 185, 186, 188, 190, 193.

All photographs by Ed Vebell, except page 7, Jim Britt; 90-91, 95, Jeff Fox; 202 (upper), Richard Pilling; 202 (lower), Stephen Szurlej; 207, Mel DiGiacomo.